T0162041

Do Protect

Legal Advice for Startups

Johnathan Rees

Published by
The Do Book Company 2014
Works in Progress Publishing Ltd
thedobook.co

A CIP catalogue record for this book
is available from the British Library

ISBN 978-1-907974-15-1

10 9 8 7 6 5 4 3 2

To find out more about our company,
books and authors, please visit
thedobook.co or follow us **@dobookco**

5% of our proceeds from the sale of
this book is given to The Do Lectures
to help it achieve its aim of making
positive change **dolectures.com**

Cover designed by James Victore
Book designed and set by Ratiotype

Printed and bound by Livonia Print Ltd

Disclaimer

No book written by a lawyer would be
complete without a disclaimer. This one
is no exception. The topics covered
here are vast and a book of this length
could not be, and is not intended to be,
a comprehensive review of the law and
practice in these areas. In my defence it
was never my intention to turn you into a
lawyer (there are too many of us already)
but rather to write a guide to the more
significant issues to be considered, from
a legal perspective, when starting a
business. You should take legal advice
before applying the information in this
book to your specific circumstances.

For my parents, Beryl and Peter.
For my daughters, Megan and Bethan.
For Johanne.

Books in the series:

Do Beekeeping
The secret to happy honeybees
Orren Fox

Do Birth
A gentle guide to labour and childbirth
Caroline Flint

Do Breathe
Calm your mind. Find focus.
Get stuff done
Michael Townsend Williams

Do Design
Why beauty is key to everything
Alan Moore

Do Disrupt
Change the status quo. Or become it
Mark Shayler

Do Fly
Find your way. Make a living.
Be your best self
Gavin Strange

Do Grow
Start with 10 simple vegetables
Alice Holden

Do Improvise
Less push. More pause. Better results.
A new approach to work (and life)
Robert Poynton

Do Lead
Share your vision. Inspire others.
Achieve the impossible
Les McKeown

Do Open
How a simple newsletter can transform
your business (and it can)
David Hieatt

Do Preserve
Make your own jams, chutneys, pickles
and cordials
Anja Dunk, Jen Goss, Mimi Beaven

Do Protect
Legal advice for startups
Johnathan Rees

Do Purpose
Why brands with a purpose do better
and matter more
David Hieatt

Do Sourdough
Slow bread for busy lives
Andrew Whitley

Do Story
How to tell your story so the world listens
Bobette Buster

Do Wild Baking
Food, fire and good times
Tom Herbert

Available in print and digital
formats from bookshops,
online retailers or via our
website: **thedobook.co**

To hear about events and forthcoming
titles, you can find us on Facebook,
on Twitter and Instagram @dobookco,
or subscribe to our newsletter

Contents

	Introduction	9
1.	Best Business Structure	13
2.	Establishing Your Website	25
3.	Intellectual Property Rights	35
4.	Raising Finance	47
5.	Dealing with Customers and Suppliers	63
6.	E-commerce and Social Media	79
7.	Building Your Team	93
8.	Essential Admin	107
9.	Selling Your Business	119
	Conclusion	133
	Resources	137
	About the Author	138
	Thanks	139
	Index	140

Introduction

Let me start by introducing myself and explaining the background to this book. I am a corporate lawyer and have been advising business startups for more than 25 years. Over that time it's fair to say that I have developed an understanding of what makes an entrepreneur and, more importantly, the hurdles and mistakes which can sabotage the best ideas and fledgling companies.

The motivation for this book was to share with you some of the experience and knowledge I have gained working with startups in the hope that this will help you lay solid foundations for your business and recognise some of the pitfalls along the way.

Do Protect has a single, simple objective – protection for entrepreneurs. From the initial decisions such as choosing the appropriate legal structure for your business to the everyday issues of dealing with customers and suppliers, raising finance and building a team, there are a variety of challenges which confront any new business – it can be all too easy to trip up. Hopefully this book will help you make the right decisions to protect you and your business.

Recent data suggests this book is relevant now more than ever. In 2013, we saw in excess of 500,000 new business registrations in the UK, continuing the growth of the last few years. Even allowing for the fact that these will not necessarily be trading immediately, this is a staggering figure – more so given the prevailing economic climate of the past five years.

Of course, there will be a variety of reasons to explain this statistic – some more positive than others – but the bottom line is, I believe, a fundamental change in people's attitude to risk. This itself is driven by different factors, but the inescapable conclusion is a growing acceptance that the world has changed. For all the threats and challenges posed, change creates opportunities for individuals not just to achieve greater flexibility and variety in their work but, in turn, to gain more control of their lives – to become masters of their own destiny. A rapidly expanding network of private investors eager to back the right businesses to plug the so-called 'equity gap' is further evidence of this trend.

Finally, a few words about what makes a successful entrepreneur. Despite what the textbooks would have you believe, in my experience there is no such thing as a typical entrepreneur. Different motivations drive different people – age, gender and experience are no indicators. That said, the most successful business startups that I have encountered are invariably led by founders who count passion and commitment among their qualities and, just as importantly, attention to detail – or at least have had someone they can rely on for that.

Like its objective, the basic message of this book is also simple. The devil always is and always will be in the detail – getting the small things right from the outset so you can then focus on the bigger picture.

So good luck with your venture. I hope this book becomes a valuable member of your team.

Law

Speaking solely as a lawyer, the United Kingdom rather unhelpfully has three different systems of law: English law (covering England and Wales and including laws made by the National Assembly for Wales), Scottish law (covering Scotland) and Northern Irish law (applicable to Northern Ireland).

For the purposes of this book the terms 'English law' or 'UK law' mean the law of England and Wales. For those of you intending to start a business in another country remember that it will be subject to its own laws taking in most of the areas covered in this book. Where applicable, you should engage local lawyers for advice. However, broadly speaking, there is much common ground between countries and my hope is that even if you are starting a business outside of the UK, this book will be of help regardless of your location.

Since this book was first published in 2014 there have been some material developments which the reader should bear in mind when reading the legal aspects covered by this book. Firstly, UK law has seen a number of regulatory changes in the areas of e-commerce and consumer protection, and secondly, the UK has voted to leave the EU. The full regulatory impact of this is, of course, unknown.

1
Best Business Structure

There are a hundred and one things to consider when you first decide to start a new business. The first and most important question, however, is how are you going to run your business? The 'how' here is not concerned with your culture or philosophy but the simple question of the type of trading structure or 'vehicle' you will use. As you will see, there are a number of options available, each involving different costs and formality – and offering varying levels of protection.

We'll look at each in more detail but the fundamental question to bear in mind is: Are you willing to be personally liable for the debts of your business?

There are of course other factors which might influence your decision, including: Will you be working alone or with others? Will each of you be equally involved in the running of the business? How do you intend to finance your business? What is your attitude to risk and exposure? However, the question of whether your assets, such as your house or flat, will be on the line invariably helps to focus the mind.

The trading structure you choose is important as the decision will affect matters ranging from your personal financial exposure to the risk perception of your business, flexibility for raising finance, levels of admin, how your business will pay its tax and how you will take money out of the business. In short, it matters.

What Are Your Options?

In essence, all business structures fall into two categories: incorporated and unincorporated. These concepts have existed in the world of commerce for a couple of centuries or more. At their core they encapsulate the two ways in which a business operates: either by trading directly with the outside world in your name 'unincorporated' or by trading indirectly through an artificial structure providing an interface between you and the outside world 'incorporated'. By way of illustration, Richard Branson trades indirectly with the outside world through his Virgin group of companies rather than directly as himself, Richard Branson.

Within these categories there are various sub-categories, but we are going to restrict ourselves to the most common, of which there are four:

Incorporated	Unincorporated
Private company limited by shares	Sole trader
Limited liability partnership (aka 'LLP')	Partnership

There are other incorporated structures – the company limited by guarantee (e.g. charities) or a limited partnership (the vehicle of choice for private equity investors) being the principal omissions – but those shown in the table above represent the most common used today.

Understanding the Different Structures

To have a better understanding of each, we are going to consider the different structures in the following areas:

— **Liability:** your financial exposure
— **Ownership:** who owns the business and how control is exercised
— **Management:** responsibility for the day-to-day running of the business
— **Admin:** formation and regulation
— **Tax**

Private company limited by shares

The limited company has been with us a long time – its origins date back to the Romans and in its present structure has been the popular vehicle of choice for commercial enterprises since the reign of Queen Victoria. There are two types of limited company: private (by far the most common and so called because they cannot offer shares to the public) and public. This book is concerned with the private version, as the vast majority of startups will begin – and many remain – private limited companies.

As students of company law discover quicker than their local bar, a company is a separate legal entity distinct from those who own and manage it. In legalese, it enjoys a 'separate legal personality'. This is at once the essence and attraction of the limited company: it is responsible for its own debts – something the parents of those students might ponder!

So why does a book proclaiming its emphasis on the practical make this seemingly academic point? If you take nothing else from this book, read and remember these two points – they go to the heart of understanding the nature of a company:

— **A company can only act through its agents – its directors – and they must act in its best interests.**

— **Ownership of the company does not mean ownership of its assets.**

This is the core of your relationship with your company. As a director, think of yourself as a custodian of your company – this will help you understand the position of trust which you hold in relation to it. Remember, you are not your company and vice versa. Blur these lines at your peril! The penalties can be severe and in the worst cases the courts will ignore the principle of separate legal personality and treat the company and its directors as one and the same – which can have devastating consequences.

Liability

Your financial exposure will be **limited** to the amount which you agree to pay in respect of your investment as a shareholder in the company. So if ownership of your company is divided into shares with a face or 'nominal' value of £1 or $1 and you agree to buy one share, your liability to the company is £1 or $1. Once you have paid that pound or dollar to the company you have no further obligation to contribute to its liabilities. To repeat, the company is liable for its own debts. All things being equal your company provides a firewall between you and the outside world. A word of caution: phrases like 'all things being equal' and 'in theory' refer euphemistically to the limited circumstances in which creditors can disregard the corporate structure and have recourse to you personally for your business's debts. However, as these will almost invariably require some wrongdoing or impropriety on your part, they are not going to receive an airing here.

Ownership
Ownership of a company is divided into individual units known as **shares**. The owners of the company are known as its **shareholders**. A share carries certain rights, e.g. to vote at company meetings, to receive a dividend when paid and ultimately for the shareholder to be repaid their investment if the company is wound up.

Management
Day-to-day management of the company's business lies with a management body who go by the name of **directors**, or collectively a **board of directors**. In the majority of UK private companies, the owners (shareholders) and managers (directors) are the same individuals – hence the term 'owner-managed business'.

Admin
Not a great selling point for the private limited company. There are a raft of matters about which a limited company must inform the Registrar of Companies (a government agency), typically relating to changes to its constitution, ownership or management. In addition, it must file a return each year of its shareholders, directors and its financial statements (which thus become a matter of public record). To these filing obligations can be added various registers which companies are required to maintain, ranging from details of the company directors and shareholders to security – mortgages and the like – created by the business in favour of its creditors. We'll expand on all this in Chapter 8.

Tax

As a separate legal entity the company is taxed on its own profits – it pays corporation rather than income tax. The double whammy is that you – whether as a manager (director) or an owner (shareholder) – will also be taxed when you take those profits out of the company as a dividend. This double taxation is one of the less appealing characteristics of a company.

One final point: there are no rules concerning the size your business must be to enjoy the status of a company.

Limited Liability Partnership (LLP)

The LLP is a relatively recent phenomenon, coming into existence in the UK only in 2000, and in the US in the early nineties (note that each individual state has its own laws governing their formation), largely in response to the plaintive cries of accountants, lawyers and other professionals (but mainly accountants) seeking protection from potentially ruinous lawsuits. An LLP is often described as a hybrid, having the external features of a company and the internal flexibility of a partnership. The point to remember again is that, as in the case of the company, the LLP is a separate legal entity and the same rules apply: the LLP owns its assets and is liable for its own debts.

Liability

While your liability as an owner or shareholder of a company is limited by the shares you hold (remember our lucky dollar?), as an owner or 'member' of an LLP your financial liability is limited to the amount which you agree to contribute and can be as large or small as you wish.

So in theory at least (those words again) if you agree to invest £20,000 to start the business that will be the limit of your liability. Again, the LLP creates a protective barrier between you and the outside world.

Ownership
The owners of the LLP are its members (commonly known as 'partners'). Unlike a company, an LLP does not have shares and you are free to set your rights (e.g. to any profits, voting rights, etc.) in agreement with your fellow members. In the absence of a formal agreement there is a statutory default mechanism which allows members to share equally in any profits.

Management
The members are free to decide how the business will be run on a day-to-day basis. In practice, most have a management board comprising a few members. That said, by law each member is able to participate in management and commit the LLP to liabilities whereas in the case of a company those rights are delegated to its directors. This makes the distinction between ownership and management easier to deal with in companies.

Admin
An LLP is subject to similar accounting and filing obligations as those applicable to a company: for example, it must file (again with the Registrar of Companies) its annual financial statements and an annual return of its members. Similarly, it must maintain registers such as a record of its members. An LLP is required to have a 'Designated Member' who has responsibility for ensuring that appropriate returns are filed and so on.

Tax

Unlike a company, an LLP does not itself pay tax. Instead the taxman looks through the LLP and taxes the members accordingly. This 'tax transparency' gives the LLP a definite advantage.

It is perhaps coincidental that a structure owing its origins to the protection of lawyers and accountants has found little popularity among the wider UK commercial community.

This brings us to the **unincorporated structures**, where the analysis becomes infinitely more straightforward.

Sole trader

This is by some margin the most common form of trading platform in the UK according to government statistics. So what do we mean by sole trader? Well, picture the scene:

Eric is sitting alone in his favourite coffee house, iPad and latte in hand, and decides he's going to do it. He's going to start a business and, moreover, he is going to do it on his own. With his word as his bond, trading in his own name with no place for the corporate interface, Eric is a sole trader. Eric has no 'firewall' between him and the outside world – he and his business are one and the same.

The upside of this structure is that Eric can start trading immediately, without any expense or formality, no on-going bureaucracy. And his financial affairs will remain private. He will own any assets he acquires for his business and he will be solely responsible for running the company, accountable to no one other than himself.

Further good news – from a tax perspective, as a sole trader Eric will be liable to income tax on the profits of his business so avoiding the 'double' taxation of a company structure.

The downside? Well, the main one is that Eric is going to be personally liable for his debts, including any lease or hire-purchase agreements he makes to acquire any of those 'assets' such as machinery, vehicles or any business premises. Of course, there is nothing to stop Eric changing his mind at a later date and turning his business into a company so he can limit these liabilities.

Partnership

Now picture a different scene. Eric is occupying that same corner seat, but this time has company. Mark and Penny are joining Eric in his new venture. And they are going to do it on their own, dealing with their customers and their suppliers, in their own names.

Eric, Mark and Penny form a partnership. They decide to call it EMPathy. They **are** their business, they own personally and equally the assets used in EMPathy and share equally the profits or losses of EMPathy, happy in the knowledge that, there being no obligations on a partnership to file financial statements, their financial affairs will remain private. As partners they will individually be responsible for paying income tax on their share of those profits – the partnership will not itself be liable to pay tax again avoiding that 'double' taxation of a company structure. As there is no requirement for any constitutional documents to be filed anywhere, they may decide to draw up an agreement between themselves, but that's for another day – and the law provides a default framework for them based upon equality, which suits them well.

The downside of this arrangement? Well Eric, Mark and Penny will each – individually – be liable for all EMPathy's debts and liabilities.

Setting Up Your Business Vehicle

Having decided upon the legal structure for your business, the next question to ask is: How to form it officially?

Company/LLP

Essentially there are two routes to formation: the first involves buying a ready-made 'off the shelf' version from formation agents; alternatively you can form your own company or LLP. The process of forming your own company can be straightforward and the costs small. In short, you will need to file an incorporation form known as form **IN01** with the Registrar of Companies providing details of the company's directors and its initial share capital, i.e. the number of shares to be taken by the founders on formation (there is no minimum or maximum) together with two documents which form its constitution:

— A **memorandum of association**, a one-page document that follows a prescribed format and states that you wish to form a company and have agreed to take the specified number of shares.

— The **articles of association**, which can follow a standard format prescribed by law (a default version) or alternatively be tailored.

The articles are essentially an agreement between the company and its members and typically deal with matters such as the creation of new shares, how shares can be sold, how directors can be appointed and the procedure for meetings of directors and shareholders. The procedure can even be done the same day, with the incorporation fee varying from £40 for a formation via the post to £14 for an internet registration.

The process and costs of forming an LLP are very similar. There are helpful websites for the procedures in establishing a company or LLP, including the British government's own website: see the Resources section at the end of the book.

Sole trader/partnership

As indicated, the procedure for establishing your business as a partnership or sole trader is straightforward: tax compliance aside (see Chapter 8), there is no procedure, and no registrations or filings are required.

Summary

So in essence the choice of trading structure comes down to three factors:

— **Personal liability**
— **Tax**
— **Raising finance**

The administrative burden and loss of privacy associated with a corporate structure (a company or LLP) is normally outweighed by the protection afforded by the limited liability status. Of course, this disregards the fact that creditors (banks, leasing companies, landlords and the like) tend to view a new company as a risky prospect and will try and protect themselves by insisting on a personal guarantee from you, the founders. Where possible, this should always be resisted.

As to the choice of corporate structure, while, as we have seen, the limited company may not tick all three boxes, its more user-friendly ownership structure and greater familiarity make it the more popular corporate vehicle. Certainly when it comes to raising finance (of which more in Chapter 4) the tax incentives available to investors give the company definite advantages and when it comes to selling – as we'll see in Chapter 9 – shares in a company are much more straightforward to deal with than a stake in an LLP. So while you will need to familiarise yourself with a director's duties and prepare yourself for the hassle of annual filings, all things being equal, the limited company will provide you with a structure that offers greater flexibility and security.

2
Establishing Your Website

Regardless of the nature of your business, chances are that your website will be a key marketing tool and your first point of contact with the outside world. As such, establishing your website will probably be one of the first things you do. Although this can now be done relatively quickly and cheaply – and you may even decide to outsource this process – it is important to remember that there are a variety of legal aspects to consider when it comes to setting up and operating a website. This chapter focuses on the legal framework and its various implications.

Of course many businesses use their website to sell their products and we deal elsewhere with online trading (Chapter 6).

Legal Framework

So what are the legal aspects, how do they impact on your website and how can you protect yourself? Well, from the choice of your domain name through to the design and content of the site and the use of visitors' data, the UK's legal system imposes a wealth of rules and regulations.

If they are breached, you and your business can be left facing fines and much worse.

Whether you set up your website using one of the many DIY facilities or engage a professional, there are a number of points to bear in mind. Here are the various stages and aspects of establishing your website:

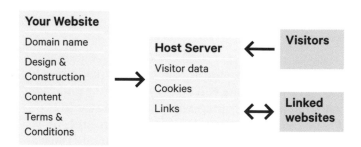

Domain name

A domain name can be a highly valuable asset ('Insure.com' was sold for $16m in 2009!) and will form part of your company identity, not least your email suffix.

Domain names break down into a number of components: take the case of my firm's domain name: www.joelsonwilson.com. The '.com' is the top level domain and indicates our type of business – in our case commercial as opposed to a governmental body, for example, which would use '.gov'. 'Joelsonwilson' is the second level and the word we have chosen (rather predictably) to identify the firm to the outside world. Finally, 'www' refers to the World Wide Web where our webpages are stored.

So what are the steps involved in choosing and registering a domain name?

First, check your preferred domain name's availability. One starting point to do this might be the WHOIS database maintained by NOMINET, which stores various information about registered domain names and their holders. NOMINET is the non-profit organisation responsible for operating the UK's national country code domain name register. The Network Solutions website is another popular starting point. Each country has its own equivalent.

Second, check whether your proposed name infringes any registered trademarks via a trademark search at the Intellectual Property Office (IPO) – the government body responsible for administrating IPR in the UK (see Resources section).

Finally, apply for registration of your domain name to NOMINET via a registrar. There are thousands of registrars – most of whom also provide webspace and hosting services – and before selecting one it would be sensible to check reviews and forums with a focus on efficiency and reliability: for example, how they handle any renewals of your domain name. As location is important, a registrar based in the country in which you'll be operating is preferable.

Website content

Your main concern will be to ensure that your layout doesn't infringe any third-party rights. For instance, in developing your site, your web designer may unwittingly (or otherwise!) be using someone else's IP if, for example, he or she failed to retain ownership of concepts and designs used in the creation of other websites. This would be unfortunate – more so if the owner of that content finds out – meaning that you could be faced with a financial claim and a request to stop using the offending content, not to mention a costly and time-consuming redesign. In short, always try and use original content.

Similarly, if you are thinking of using an endorsement from a satisfied customer, tread carefully. First and foremost it must be authentic (inventing one runs the risk of committing a criminal offence). Secondly, make sure that you have the relevant permission, not just for the quote, but also a customer's logo if you are reproducing it.

Data

Your website is likely to collect a variety of data on visitors ranging from their name, contact and credit card details to their online behaviour. The capture and use of that information will fall within the UK's data protection regime: the Data Protection Act 1998 (DPA). In short, anyone processing personal information electronically must notify the Information Commissioner's Office (ICO) before they do so, unless they are exempt. Failure to notify when required is a criminal offence and, even if exempt, the DPA contains a number of regulations which you will need to observe.

The ICO has a helpful website (see Resources) with guidance on whether you need to register as a data controller and some useful training materials. For startups and smaller businesses the costs of registration are nominal (£35, renewable annually) and the level of information required about your business is limited.

A couple of points: 'processing' includes obtaining and storing information and 'personal information' means any details about individuals which can be used to identify them and need not be confidential.

These obligations fall on the 'data controller' rather than the actual processor, who might not be the same person (say if you have outsourced your IT functions). The likelihood is that, as the person with the ability to determine the purpose for which the information is used, you will be the controller.

As breaches of the legislation can result in criminal as well as civil liability (not to mention untold reputational damage) it would be unwise to ignore your obligations in this area.

Links to other sites

You will need to check the terms of any website which you propose to link to from your site. While links are generally welcomed by other businesses, website owners will want to protect themselves against links to sites which could harm it commercially and so may well impose conditions (usually apparent from their website) on any such linking. One further point: a link licence would not include the right to use that third party's trademarks and so you would need to address that separately. The simplest option is to email and ask the business or individual if they have any objection to your linking through.

Links to your site

In the same way, it would be prudent to regulate how and when others can link to your website. To do so, you will need to ensure that you have a linking licence in place ideally in 'click-wrap' form so that any linker must actively 'accept' your terms. Make sure your licence is specific and stops the linker doing anything which might harm your business.

Business information

There are a raft of regulations which govern the information about your business that must be displayed on your website, including the full company name, registered number and registered office. Many sites have this on a separate page of 'legal information' so the look and feel of the site isn't compromised.

Website terms and conditions

Your website should include terms and conditions covering access to and use of your site. Matters for you to consider include:

— **Restrictions** on use of the content of the site (e.g. print and downloadable extracts).

— A statement that all **rights** in the website belong to you (or the relevant third party, e.g. where your site uses someone else's content).

— Obligations on visitors not to post any illegal or harmful **content** on the site. In addition to the reputational risk, you could face third-party claims for infringement of their rights (see Chapter 6).

— Terms for **linking** to your site.

— Obligations not to transfer any **passwords** necessary to access your site.

— A **disclaimer** for the content or performance of the website.

— Reference to your **privacy policy**. This will set out your business's practice on the collection, storage and use of personal data and **cookies**.

Finally, take care to ensure that your visitor has accepted your terms – again, more of which in Chapter 6.

Cookies

Akin to a form of ID, a cookie (a small file of numbers and letters) will distinguish a visitor from other users of your site. Cookies have a range of purposes, from allowing the user access to your site (to browse, order, etc.) to analysing information about them and tracking their interest in your products. It was this notion of 'Big Brother' – storing information about users – which attracted concern and led to changes in the law. Now, users must be properly informed about the cookies used on your site, their purpose and, importantly, must give their consent (to the holding of their data captured by the cookies). So your website should contain a clear and prominent cookie policy notice. The visitor can then be deemed to have consented even if they omit to tick the relevant box and move to another page. We look at the subject of cookies in more detail in Chapter 6.

Summary

Although your website is an important sales and marketing tool for your business, do not forget that it can also expose your business. Whether in its design, content or the use of information about your site's visitors, there are a number of legal and regulatory aspects that can trip the unwary. As a minimum, a comprehensive set of website terms and conditions will go a long away to protecting you from any pitfalls.

3
Intellectual Property Rights

Intellectual property (IP) is fundamentally concerned
with ideas and the expression of them whether in
writing, film or other mediums. There is, as they say,
a clue in the title, and the law has evolved to classify
both the different assets which come under this umbrella
term and the procedures in place for their protection.

Every business starts with an idea, but it is important to
understand that it is not the idea that is protected but how
it is articulated. In order for an idea to be protected it has to
exist in one of the recognised formats in which intellectual
property rights exist. Put another way, if you have a great
idea it will only be protected if you don't tell anyone (so no
one can copy it) or you set it down in some recorded format.

It follows that every business that articulates its idea
owns IP or, put another way, rights in IP (IPR) – we will
use these terms interchangeably. To some this statement
is obvious, but to many starting out the importance and
value of their ideas can be overlooked. So whether you are
selling a brand-new product or simply your know-how,
this is an important subject for all startups.

In essence IPR are the bricks and mortar of a brand or
content led business. As creator, you have the right to stop

others copying your idea and, depending on the type of IP, an exclusive right to commercialise it.

So, in this chapter we will:

— Look at the different types of intellectual property.

— Help you to recognise those assets within your own business and who owns them.

— Explain the importance of the protection of those assets, how to register them, and the enforcement of those rights.

— Analyse briefly the different ways which your business might exploit its IPR.

There are a myriad of textbooks and resources dealing with the process of the registration of IPR, the protection that exists automatically, and the criteria to be satisfied – something beyond the scope of this book. But a general word of caution: those who have been through the process of registering their IP will tell you that it can be both complex and expensive especially if it is not thought through or budgeted for at the start.

Types of IPR

So what do we mean by intellectual property?

A typical business will own assets which are both physical or tangible, such as property, machinery, vehicles, and so on, and other assets that are non-physical or intangible. IP falls into this second category.

In the UK, IPR can be registered or unregistered. In other words, rights which are capable of protection by registration (with a governmental agency) and those which can be protected in other ways or are protected automatically on creation. These can be summarised broadly as follows:

Registered	Unregistered
Patents	Copyright
Trademarks	Design rights
Registered designs	Confidential information

Firstly, let's take a look at those types that can be registered.

Patents

These protect a new or novel invention and enable the inventor to stop others from copying, making, selling or using that invention by registering it and describing how the invention works. Well-known recent examples include the Apple iPad and the Dyson vacuum cleaner. There is another aspect to registration, namely the publicity which accompanies an application. A former colleague would frequently remind clients (much to the chagrin of his partners, who saw only lost fees) that the application process would invariably enable competitors to see how their invention worked. The risk is that third parties – particularly large corporates who monitor this sort of thing – are able to develop with a few tweaks a competing product without infringing your invention. So it's not just the monetary cost of the exercise which needs to be considered. It's also the exposure and increased risk of copycats.

Trademarks

These cover a wide variety of identifying features: logos (the Adidas stripes, McDonalds' arches, Apple's apple), colours (Cadbury's purple), brand names (Nike), shapes (the Coca-Cola bottle), slogans and strap-lines ('The future's bright, the future's...'), sounds (the roar of the MGM lion) and even smells! Trademarks are used to distinguish the goods or services offered by your business from those offered by another so trademarks protect the goodwill and reputation in a business.

You can have registered and unregistered trademarks. Unregistered trademark rights are not easily enforceable but they have value, as they may give you the right to claims in 'passing off' – for example if a third party does something the same or similar to your business and in doing so misrepresents itself, creates confusion and causes damage. The value in unregistered marks lies in the rights to prevent this type of misleading conduct.

Registered trademarks are recorded at a registry (more of which below) against the business's goods or services. Trademarks are registered in 'classes' (with a fee payable for each class) depending on the type of goods or service they relate to and there is a fee payable for each class. There are some 45 classes and you should be aware that registering your trademark in one class won't necessarily prevent a third party from registering the same mark in a different class unless there is a likelihood of confusion. That said the classes are broad and the registration process will help guide you to the relevant class(es) for your product or service.

Registered designs

The aim of design rights in their broader sense,
i.e. registered and unregistered designs, is to protect
the appearance of a product. A registered design is
concerned with the 'look and feel' of your product and
protects its visual appearance, e.g. its colour, texture
or shape. It is a monopoly right, so it will give you the
exclusive right to make your product and allow you to
sue for infringement – even where the alleged wrongdoer
created the same design entirely independently (in other
words, they claim they didn't copy it).

Now let's move on to unregistered intellectual
property rights.

Design rights

In fast-moving markets such as the fashion industry,
unregistered design rights have become a useful defence
for designers where the time and cost of registration of
a design make the process unviable. While registered
designs are concerned more with the aesthetic (external),
design rights are typically concerned with both the
external and the internal, i.e. shape and functionality.

Design rights can only protect designs in 3-D form,
so a fashion designer looking to protect a 2-D image on its
latest accessory would have to register the design or rely
on copyright. In essence, protection lasts for the lesser of
15 years from creation of the design or 10 years from first
sale. Unlike a registered design it is not a 'monopoly' right,
so infringement only occurs if the design is actually copied
(i.e. it can't prevent a product being produced which
innocently includes your design).

Copyright

Copyright arises on the creation of the work. It is instant and does not require registration or any additional formality. The more important question is who created the work and who owns it. This is of fundamental importance for businesses and the development of their assets.

It lasts for the lifetime of the creator and 70 years after his or her death, or, in the case of sound recordings and broadcasts, 50 years from publication. It is important to remember that copyright doesn't protect an idea but the expression of that idea. In a commercial context, copyright can exist in databases, reports and technical drawings, for example an architect's drawings, computer software, plans, websites and webcasts.

Confidential information

Although not IP in the conventional sense, it is common for businesses to generate information that is commercially sensitive and if disclosed could harm the business. Almost any type of information can be confidential including your business's finances, customer lists and marketing plans.

English law has long recognised the principle that a person receiving such information in confidence can't exploit it if they knew or should have known they were under a duty to keep it secret. This may be obvious where the other party has signed an agreement, but the duty to keep information confidential can arise in other situations, e.g. because of the nature of the relationship (e.g. employer/employee) or where the information is shared in a way which makes it clear it is not to be disclosed. That said, there is no doubt that implying an obligation of confidentiality in this way is difficult and you have much greater protection if there is an agreement in place.

Of course, it is quite possible, even likely, that your business will generate a combination of these different intellectual property rights. And there may well be an overlap in that the same idea can create more than one IPR.

Ownership of IPR

Ownership of IPR is key when considering its protection, enforcement and exploitation, and also in the context of any fund-raising for your business.

The general rule is that the creator is the first owner – though there are a few exceptions. The first is that employees do not own the IPR (most often copyright) in work they create in the course of their employment. This is of crucial importance and must be distinguished from the potentially frightening reality that works created by a person who is not an actual employee will belong to that person NOT the person paying for the work. If that is the case a business may find that it doesn't own the IPR in its own products but instead has an implied licence to use them for a limited purpose. Clearly this could be extremely harmful to the business; the position can only be avoided by something expressed in writing to the contrary and signed by the creator before or after the work is done. All freelancers working for your company should therefore sign written agreements transferring rights to your business (as the commissioner).

These are the sort of issues which can become problematic when looking for investment or licensing your IP – or indeed selling your business.

A word of caution: if you or your colleagues have undertaken any work in relation to the development of your brand before forming your business, it would be sensible to formally transfer any such rights to the new business to avoid any confusion at a later date.

Recognising Your IPR

This is your starting point. There will be some elements which are more obvious than others:

— Your chosen trading name should be protected by registration at Companies House (regardless of whether you are operating as a limited company) and you should also consider whether to register it as a trademark.

— You may have a logo which can be protected as a trademark.

— Your chosen domain name and website will also form part of your 'brand' and will need to be registered (see Chapter 2).

— Your business's day-to-day activities may generate IPR. Obvious examples are inventions or designs, but there may be more subtle non-registrable rights such as know-how (e.g. recipes) which are key to your business.

How to Register Your IPR

Where your IP is capable of registration then, if you can afford it, the prudent course is to do so. How you do this depends on the type of IP.

Trademarks

A UK trademark application would be made to the IPO (Intellectual Property Office – see Resources) and a first step would be to conduct an online search either yourself or using a trademark specialist to ensure that your mark, patent or design is not already registered. There is an online application procedure which can be followed and the IPO has a helpful website which sets out the process, timescale and fees payable. As the owner of a trademark you can apply for UK- or EU-wide protection – both registrations run for 10 years and can be renewed for 10-year periods. As mentioned earlier, you will need to identify the classes in which you wish to register. You can apply to register your trademark immediately – there is no need to have started trading.

The timescale for registration will vary (depending on the complexity of the mark) but it is possible to obtain a UK registration in a few months if there are no objections or opposition. The IPO currently charges £200 for a UK trademark application, plus £50 for any additional classes in which you wish to register your mark.

Remember that registering your trademark in the UK won't give you protection elsewhere. If your business is international you can protect your trademark overseas in one of three ways:

— **Nationally** in an individual country by application to the relevant registry in that country.

— **Throughout Europe** by way of a European trademark (a community trademark or CTM) via the Office for Harmonisation in the Internal Market (OHIM) based in Spain, or alternatively via the relevant national trademark office. If you are looking to do business in Europe it may be more cost effective to start with the EU first, as an EU mark, while being more expensive, will cover the UK and all the other EU member countries.

— **Worldwide** through the World Intellectual Property Organisation (WIPO) under the Madrid Protocol, which will extend protection for your mark to all those states which are a party to the protocol.

Overseas protection can be complex and you would be well advised to engage professional assistance if you decide to pursue this route.

If you want to engage a specialist to manage the process for you there will be a cost but you can often get a fixed fee so you know the full cost up front.

Patents

UK protection: A similar process to that for trademarks applies, though one important point to remember when registering a patent is that a previous disclosure of the information may prevent registration. To reduce this risk, those involved in the creation of your product (potential investors, manufacturers, freelancers and the like) should be asked to sign confidentiality agreements, the invention should not be publiciy exposed and you should consider filing a patent application for the invention in advance of any disclosure. An application must be filed with the IPO and once granted protection lasts for 20 years. Beware: patent protection is expensive and the bar for registration is set high.

The timescale for obtaining a UK patent can typically be anywhere between two and four years.

Remember that as with trademarks so a patent registration in the UK will not protect you overseas. Where you are looking for international protection for your invention there are a few different routes you might take:

— You might apply via the European Patent Convention (EPC) which is administered by the Munich-based European Patent Office. A single application is made to the EPO designating the countries in which you are seeking protection. Ultimately this leads to the grant of a European patent which operates as a collection of separate patents in each of the relevant countries.

— If you need protection in only a few European countries you can apply for protection to the relevant national office.

— Alternatively for wider protection application can be made under the Patent Co-operation Treaty (PCT) which is administered by the WIPO. If you are based in the UK a single application is made with the IPO – the UK's national registry – which effectively includes all the countries within the PCT on the application date. Each application then proceeds separately in each country that is a party to the treaty.

A couple of final points. A new European patent is being introduced (a 'unitary patent') simplifying both application and enforcement procedures. It also is worth pointing out that the UK corporate tax system can provide relatively generous tax rates for profits generated from protected IPR and reliefs for research and development costs and, if relevant, this is an area where you would be well advised to seek specialist tax advice.

Registered designs

You can apply to the IPO to protect your design as a registered design any time within the first 12 months of the design being 'disclosed'. This grace period gives you time to gauge the commercial potential and whether registration and the related time and cost implications are economically viable.

Confidential information

Where possible this should be protected by appropriate contracts, e.g. in employment contracts and consultancy agreements, to ensure that individuals and organisations engaged by your business are prevented from leaking or sharing sensitive company information. Similarly, when talking to potential collaborators or investors it would be prudent to require them to sign confidentiality agreements (aka non-disclosure agreements or NDAs). The cynical view is that NDAs aren't worth the paper they're written on, as once disclosure is made the damage is done and proving the breach is challenging. But there is no doubt that an NDA discourages casual disclosure and makes your business look more professional when approaching investors.

Obviously you'll need to take a view on when it is appropriate to produce an NDA. If you're working with people you already know, introducing such a document could raise a trust issue and that might not go down too well.

Enforcing Your IPR

The ability to enforce your IPR is central to preserving its value by deterring would-be copycats and counterfeiters, and preventing IP leakage and, in turn, preventing lost revenue, which can be extremely damaging for new businesses.

The basic remedies available regardless of the nature of your IPR are:

— **Damages** (financial compensation)
— **Injunction** (stopping the infringer from making further copies of your product)
— **Hand-over or destruction** of infringing products

Regrettably, all of these involve engaging lawyers and petitioning the courts. Depending on the strength of your position, it may be that you can achieve your goals without a time-consuming and expensive court process, instead relying upon specialist lawyers who can help you not only achieve redress but also recover their costs from the infringer at the same time!

It is safe to say that your position is strengthened where your IPR has been registered, but at the very least it will be vital for you to have records to prove ownership of your IPR.

Exploiting Your IPR

Having created and, where possible, protected your IPR, you'll now be thinking about how to commercialise it. There are several options open to you to generate income:

— **License others to use it:** this would typically generate royalties payable by your licensee. You would retain ownership of the IPR and, depending upon the terms of the licence, be free to award licences to other organisations.

— **Sell it:** alternatively you might decide to transfer ownership of your IP to generate a one-off sum.

— **Use it as security for a loan:** if the lender sees sufficient value in your IP (the likelihood is that it would need to be registered IP) it may be prepared to lend your business money against some form of collateral based on it.

Summary

Intellectual property can form an integral part of your business's brand and strategy. Properly understood and managed it can give you a competitive edge, helping you to grow market share, generate revenue and so ultimately enhance the value of your business.

It is essential that you understand exactly what IPR exists in your business, and that you take whatever appropriate steps you can to protect it and extract full value from it. This may not necessarily mean registration in the first instance but, if nothing else, make sure that your partners acknowledge where ownership lies, particularly where you are involved in any form of collaboration.

4
Raising Finance

Having decided to start your own business, I'm sure that part of your planning will have addressed money and the question of how the business will be funded. You may well be looking for an investor. When we refer to an 'investor' here we are describing any person – a bank, friend, relative, stranger or experienced entrepreneur – who is thinking of putting money into your business in one form or another.

This can be an intimidating arena for any entrepreneur, not least because they typically find themselves in a weak bargaining position and drawn into discussions which can range from awkward to downright humiliating. Negotiating for funding will involve you in selling three key elements to your investor:

— **You:** your commitment, passion and vision.

— **Your idea:** proof that your business concept works ('proof of concept' in the jargon), is protected or capable of protection (IPR – see Chapter 3) and it is scalable.

— **Your financial model:** your financial projections are credible and can withstand scrutiny.

Few of us enjoy selling – and even fewer enjoy selling ourselves or our ideas. While there is no substitute for thorough preparation (you must understand your business and its potential markets inside out) the most important factor for any investor will be you. So while you may not need to be Warren Buffett-like with your grasp of the 'numbers', it would be sensible to know someone who is and can deal with the difficult financial questions that will come your way during the investment process.

Types of Funding

Essentially there are two types of funding, each having different legal implications (the profits you make and re-invest in your business are a third):

— **Debt:** a loan of some description where money is invested in your business on a temporary basis on the understanding that it is repaid to the investor over an agreed timeframe.

— **Equity:** where the cash investment takes a more permanent form usually as capital (in the case of a sole trader, partnership or LLP) or shares (in the case of a company).

From a legal and practical perspective these are very different creatures and will dictate the nature of the relationship between you and your investor.
The essential differences between the two are the degree of risk which the investor accepts and the potential upside they might enjoy:

	Debt	Equity
Risk	Typically secured; ranks ahead of equity investors in the event of insolvency	No security; entirely at risk
Timescale	Short term; typically repaid in 2 to 5 years	Long term; cannot be repaid except in limited circumstances

The equity investor therefore has a much bigger interest in your company's success.

Debt (or loan)

For startups, this may be a business loan via a bank or government agency. Here the debt investor or lending body will be primarily concerned with:

— Getting repaid the amount of the investment (the **principal**).
— Obtaining a return on the investment in the meantime (the **interest**).
— What collateral is available to help recover the investment if you fail to repay it (the **security**).

For the loan provider, the best outcome is getting their money back and being paid the agreed interest. The success of your business is welcome but they do not participate in it beyond this limited return. Cash is very much king for them. Be warned: the loan repayments can start almost immediately – in some cases before trading has even begun – and carrying debt from the outset is not the most uplifting way to start your business.

Equity

Equity investors, on the other hand, are looking at you and your business very differently and are more concerned with your longer-term success because they plan to participate in it. The equity investor's primary concerns will relate to:

— Growth in the value of their investment ('**capital appreciation**').
— The ability to realise their investment (an '**exit**').
— The ability to influence affairs if the business starts to struggle.

They may also wish to receive a regular return on their investment in the form of a dividend, but this is often a secondary issue for equity investors in new businesses.

Retained Profits

It is commonly accepted that any profits generated during the business's early years are best used by being reinvested in the business, as this is the cheapest form of funding for any business. Profits reinvested in this way are known as 'retained profits'.

Sources of Funding

Let's look at possible funding sources depending on the type of investment you're looking for.

Debt (or loan)

The most obvious source is, of course, your bank manager (the prefix 'friendly' was dropped some time ago). This may or may not be the bank holding your personal account, though if it is this may help the conversation. While in theory there is no reason why a private investor should not consider offering you a loan, in practice it isn't a particularly attractive option for them – especially if they are looking to obtain some form of tax relief on their investment.

In addition to the high street banks there are a variety of specialist lenders, such as government agencies who lend specifically to startups. And a relatively recent and fast-growing phenomenon is the concept of peer-to-peer or 'social' lending.

Banks

There are two types of loan (or 'facility') that a bank will typically provide: an overdraft (repayable on demand), and a loan repayable over a set period (usually two to five years) known as a 'term loan'. As an overdraft can be withdrawn by the bank at any time, the term loan represents a more stable form of funding. The main elements of the loan arrangement will comprise:

— **The amount the bank is prepared to lend**, commonly known as 'the principal'.

— **The interest you will have to pay** on that principal (usually deductible against your profits).

— **The dates on which the loan is repayable** (typically at monthly intervals by direct debit). It is certainly much less complicated for a bank to be repaid its loan than it is for an investor's equity to be returned.

— **The security for the loan.** If the business already has assets and these are perceived by the bank as having value, then the bank will take security over them. That way, if you cannot make the repayments, the loan provider knows it can realise those assets to recover its debt.

Be pragmatic when applying for a bank loan. Banks are not keen on altering their small-print-laden documents, so beyond ensuring that the main terms are as agreed, don't expect to negotiate terms.

As startups are seldom synonymous with meaningful security, most banks – if they are inclined to lend to a startup at all – will request a personal guarantee from you as the founder, often secured by your home as collateral.

If you are a sole trader this may be less of an issue. You will recall from Chapter 1 that you are personally liable for your business's debts anyway, so the only question is whether you are prepared to give the bank a charge over your home. As it is probably already mortgaged, there will be questionable value in this for the bank and if the house is in joint names (e.g. with a spouse or partner) then there are procedures (and paperwork) that the bank has to follow carefully.

If you have formed a company (or indeed an LLP) as your business structure then beware – a personal guarantee is the way in which that much-vaunted limited liability is cunningly circumvented by the bank! In short, if you can decline any guarantee request, try to do so.

Peer-to-peer lending

This is very similar in concept to crowdfunding (more of which in the 'Equity' section), in that borrowers are connected to savers (lenders) through internet-based intermediaries, the investment being in the form of a loan. The concept has grown rapidly and has received the support of the UK government, not least because it provides an alternative to traditional bank funding. The form and terms of your loan will be in a standard form and dealt with by the relevant intermediary.

Government schemes

There are a number of government sources for SMEs (small to medium enterprises). When launched, the Business Bank (see Resources) may provide another funding opportunity in the UK. It will provide funding to small business lenders and is likely to consolidate all existing government funding schemes.

Equity

There are a number of sources of potential equity investors; some of the more obvious are:

— **Friends and family** – though to borrow my old senior partner's favourite maxim: it is better to make friends of your investors than investors of your friends.

— **Customers or suppliers** of your business.

— **Business angels:** wealthy entrepreneurs who have run and sold their own businesses. There are a number of angel networks but a good starting point would be the UK Business Angels Association (see Resources).

— **Venture capitalists:** there are many venture capital firms in the US and the UK, take a look at The British Venture Capital Association (BVCA, see Resources).

— **Corporate venturers:** large companies with surplus cash have established their own funds with a view to investing in smaller growing businesses and making a better return than putting the money on deposit with their bank.

— **Crowdfunding:** the raising of money from the public via internet-based platforms has become an established mode of capital raising for young and developing businesses with a variety of investment types, from P2P lending to donations and rewards based funding through to equity investments. There are a number of legal and regulatory aspects which a business needs to consider and the platform provider – of which there are many – will help provide guidance.

— **Government:** there are a number of government sources for small businesses depending on their maturity ranging from the Enterprise Capital Funds to the Business Growth Fund.

In addition, generous UK tax reliefs in the form of the Enterprise Investment Scheme and the Seed Enterprise Investment Scheme are available to equity investors in certain qualifying small businesses. The procedures must be followed carefully but the schemes can be a significant incentive for potential investors.

Crowdfunding: A few practical observations

— **More than cash:** As well as raising the profile of your business, a well-run process allows your customers and suppliers to become stakeholders (and brand ambassadors) and brings you into contact with more experienced investors who can help with business development.

— **Be prepared:** The process can typically take between 2 and 4 months and will be time-consuming. Pre-launch will involve dealing with the platform provider, legal documents, pitch presentation and marketing – you should alert your community to the initiative before you launch.

— **Be organised:** Post-launch you will have to respond to investor questions. Try and identify these in advance, save answers and automate business plan requests. Ensure that you follow up conversations and deal with all investor queries.

— **Be savvy:** Before you launch, try and secure investor commitments to get your campaign off to a good start. Post-launch, identify the larger investors and prioritise your efforts.

— **Be realistic:** Set your minimum fundraising target sensibly. 'FOMO' (fear of missing out) often sees investments surge once that is reached.

— **Do negotiate:** Platform providers' costs typically range between 4 – 7% of funds raised. Try and negotiate the commission rate, especially when investors have been introduced by you before launch.

What an Equity Investor Looks for

So what will your investor be looking for when considering their investment?

Whatever the nature of the investment you are seeking, the starting point is your business plan. There are hundreds of books out there on this subject and this isn't one of them. However, you can assume that while a good business plan won't guarantee that you get your money, a poor one will guarantee you won't.

The investor will focus on a range of matters:

— **You:** your experience, commitment, vision and focus and in particular any gaps in your skills which need to be covered.

— **Your sector:** it is likely that the investor (particularly of the 'angel' variety) will be keener to invest in a sector of which they have experience.

— **Your market:** barriers to entry, the competition, your business's unique selling point, and whether that market is growing.

— **Your strategy:** how are you going to achieve and deliver your vision?

The Equity Investment Process

This will vary according to the type of investor. Typically the process starts with the issue of a 'taster' document by you: this will be a brief summary of your business proposition, the amount you are looking to raise and the purpose of the investment.

A word of caution: strict rules surround this type of document, i.e. anything intended to induce someone to buy shares in your business. The taster document would constitute a 'financial promotion' and as such you will need to ensure that the person you are approaching falls within one of the exemptions to the rules, e.g. is a 'high net worth individual' or a 'sophisticated investor'. This is a complex but vital area and the bottom line is to make sure you are properly advised!

If the potential investor is interested then normally a few meetings would follow giving the investor an opportunity to get to know you (and vice versa) and understand your business proposition.

If the investor remains keen then it would be sensible to draw up **heads of terms** (a brief summary of the main terms) or for the investor to issue a letter setting out the terms of their offer. This document would not be legally binding on you or the investor and would deal with high-level issues such as:

— **The amount** the investor is prepared to invest.

— **The percentage of equity** they will receive in return.

— **The conditions to the investment** – typically checks ('due diligence') to be run on you and your business/concept.

The Investment Document

Finally, assuming that the hurdles have been jumped successfully (and you and the investor are still on speaking terms), the investor will typically engage a lawyer to set out the terms of their investment. Again, this is an important but broad topic and you too should engage a lawyer to check the agreement – preferably one with some experience of this type of transaction. The key issues for you as the investee will be:

- **The amount and timing of the investment** (single payment or instalments?).

- **The financial return required by the investor** (e.g. dividend rights).

- **Vetoes** (decisions which will need the investor's approval). This negotiation will give you an indication of how 'hands on' your investor is likely to be.

- **Reporting and governance** (the amount of financial information required and at what intervals; will the investor be on the board?).

- **The warranties that the investor requires** (assurances by you about your proposition). These are significant in that if the statements prove to be untrue the investor may have a financial claim against you.

- **Any provisions forcing you to sell your shares** if you are no longer employed in the business and – importantly – the price you will receive for those shares.

- **The right of the investor to force you to sell your shares** alongside them if a buyer emerges and vice versa.

It may be that the investor will require you to enter into a formal contract of employment with your business to ensure that you are properly tied in; similarly, if your business relies on any intellectual property rights, the investor will want to ensure that these belong to the company, which may in turn involve you or other third parties transferring such rights to the business as a condition of the investment.

It is important to remember that much of what is in the legal documentation is standard across the private equity industry and there is little to be gained from seeking to negotiate every point.

Choosing Your Equity Investor

There are a number of things to keep in mind if you are fortunate enough to have a choice of investors:

— **Look beyond the cash:** ideally the investor will have experience in your sector and have connections (e.g. potential suppliers and customers) to help develop your business.

— **Deep pockets:** consider the investor's ability to commit more funds.

— **Chemistry:** do you get on? You are likely to see a fair bit of each other, so this is important.

— **Hands on:** how involved in the day-to-day running of the business does your investor want to be; what vetoes are required by the investor? To put it another way, what level of interference you can expect?

— **Flexibility:** how much freedom do you have to raise additional equity finance? Can the investor block it or do they merely have the right to participate and protect their equity percentage? What if you want to award shares to staff?

— **Expectations:** when does the investor anticipate being able to realise their investment? Do they see it as a long-term venture? If so, does this suit you?

— **Cost of the investment:** This is not just the percentage of equity which the investor demands and which will determine the capital sum they receive when they sell, but also the income they require in respect of that investment in the meantime. This would typically take the form of dividends and non-executive director or consultancy fees. On which note remember: most growing small businesses prefer to reinvest profits rather than pay out dividends – an experienced investor should not expect much by way of dividends for the first few years of his investment.

— **Equity split:** this is a notoriously difficult discussion for a startup when the debate is happening before the true value of the business is known. It's your business and you don't want to feel like you're working for your investor from the get-go. The need for cash can make it all too easy for you to concede too much equity but no prudent investor will want a demotivated management team. It would be sensible to have a clear idea of the amount of equity (e.g. 70 per cent) that you want to be set aside for you and your management team – existing and future. As a compromise you might also consider a mechanism allowing you to increase your equity share once the investor achieves an agreed return on their investment.

Summary

Raising the appropriate form of finance for your business can make all the difference. The market for debt funding is challenging for small businesses and that is unlikely to change any time soon.

By contrast, raising equity, especially from the right source, can provide both stability for your business and a launch pad. The equity funding process can be exciting, challenging and time-consuming, but there are a few basic rules to keep in mind during negotiations.

First, respect the process. It always pays to try and see things from the investor's perspective. However sure you are that your business is going to fly, this is a high-risk investment for them. It follows that the investor is likely to want to gain as much information about you, the business and its market as possible.

Second, keep calm. Remember that after the negotiations are out of the way your on-going relationship with your investor is key, so make sure you keep discussions professional.

Third, remember that the agreements will be legally binding, so don't be fooled into thinking that once signed they will be placed in a drawer, never to see the light of day again. Rest assured, they will – particularly if the business is not performing or there is disagreement on the way forward. So choose your battles carefully and focus on the key commercial aspects we have outlined.

Finally, keep it simple. My experience suggests an unfortunate correlation between complex negotiations and unsuccessful investments.

5
Dealing with Customers and Suppliers

The most fundamental aspect of running your business will be generating cash and making a profit. This process will, of course, involve buying materials and services from suppliers and in turn selling your goods or services to customers. These arrangements are the essence of any business; however good your product or service, getting these relationships right can determine whether you succeed or fail. In this chapter we are going to focus on:

— The legal aspects of dealings with your customers and suppliers, i.e. your contracts for purchase on the one hand and sale on the other.

— The different routes to selling your product or services to your customers.

From trading contracts to staff contracts and even the purchase of your gas and electricity, the daily running of your business will involve a multitude of arrangements and dealings. The first and fundamental point to understand is that each of these dealings will be a **contract** – and understanding what that means is the principal objective of this chapter.

To use a game as an analogy, the key issues for you when entering into an agreement with your customer or supplier are to ensure that:

— You decide when the game starts, in other words when the contract – and its legally binding obligations – comes into existence.

— You get to write, or at least understand, the rules of the game or in other words the terms of that contract.

— It is clear when the game ends, i.e. when the contract comes to an end and you must pay or are entitled to be paid.

Having set the context, let's start right at the beginning with an explanation of some basic terms and concepts.

What Is a Contract?

A contract is essentially an agreement between two parties that can be enforced in a court. Its existence means that you or your customer/supplier can seek redress from the courts if the other party reneges on its side of the deal. That action will essentially take the form of a claim for financial compensation ('damages') for the wrong committed (the 'breach') and/or a direction by the court that the defaulting side honours its part of the agreement.

A common misconception is that a contract needs to be signed in ink, in the presence of witnesses, bound by a pink ribbon and sealed with red wax. Not so. A contract requires little formality, indeed it doesn't need to exist in the physical sense at all (English law recognises oral agreements). Unfortunately, this informality can be both a help and a hindrance – not least because when it comes to the terms of any contract it is important to remember that they come with a number of 'default settings', more of which below.

Let the Games Begin!
When Is Your Contract Formed?

Understanding when a legally binding commitment has arisen is essential because this determines when you and your customer/supplier become legally bound to buy/supply your/their products.

Under English law the general position is that a contract comes into being upon an 'offer' being accepted – the offer typically being made by the seller and accepted by the buyer. Up to that point either of you is, in principle, free to walk away. You will not be surprised to learn that this topic could be a book in itself, but for our purposes let's say that for a contract to exist you and your customer/supplier must have reached the stage where both parties intend to be legally bound and the terms of the arrangement are sufficiently clear.

There are a variety of reasons why the 'start' can be confused. The most common is that there is no agreement between you and your customer/supplier as to when negotiations have stopped and a contract has started. For example, it is not uncommon for a plethora of emails and phone calls to pass between you and the other party and then segue into a binding contract without one (or perhaps either) of you realising it.

The solution is to cover the point in your standard conditions so that you are under no obligation to do anything until you say so, and obtain a written confirmation from your customer/supplier acknowledging that fact. In other words, no contract comes into being, and the game doesn't start, until you have this in place.

Rules of the Game:
The Terms of Your Contract

So, having established that you need to have some control over when a contract comes into being, the next question is: What will the contract look like? A contract comes into being with a number of default settings – 'terms' which are agreed between you and the customer/supplier; incorporated by your customer/supplier (cunningly or otherwise) or, ultimately, imposed by a court in the event of a dispute from a variety of sources – the moral of this story is to try and influence these terms. In other words, to write the rules of the game. Whatever the nature of your business, it is good practice to have a standard set of conditions which will cover the sale of your goods (or supply of your services) so that, in the absence of anything you agree to the contrary, they will apply to all your dealings with customers.

The alternative is to discover that the contract to supply is subject to your customer's conditions supplemented by some unwelcome default provisions, the grand effect of which is that you have unwittingly accepted obligations and liabilities which are unlikely to be in your favour.

This area is often complicated by the so-called 'battle of the forms', where a series of communications pass between you and your counter-party – both parties attempting to ensure that your respective terms and conditions will govern the contract. There is a view that firing off the last shot in this exchange before the contract comes into being wins the day, but the safe course is to ensure that your customer/supplier acknowledges that your terms prevail before you start work or deliver the goods.

Customers

So, what are the things you should include in your contract with a customer? The principal areas will be:

— When you will become legally bound to supply your goods or services.

— What you have agreed to do: this is key to avoiding confusion about when the contract comes to an end and you can chase payment.

— Your potential liability: as far as possible you should limit your liability under the contract, while recognising that there are complex rules as to what can and can't be excluded (a specialist area which you will need to take advice on).

— The price payable by the customer and what is included, e.g. exclusive of taxes and shipping costs, etc.

— Payment terms and protection for late payment (charging interest perhaps) or non-payment (reserving ownership of your products pending payments).

— Ensuring that any IP in your product belongs to you, particularly where you have been approached specifically by the customer to make or design a product or service for them.

— One final point: you would be well advised to draw-up standard terms and conditions which will apply to all your dealings with customers. Engaging a lawyer will help you tailor them to your business.

Collecting your cash

Customer issues invariably tend to arise only when it comes to payment. There is nothing more frustrating than performing your part of the bargain only to find your customer withholding payment – frequently using you as a form of finance for their business – whether it is 'can't pay' or, more ominously, 'won't pay'. Either way, cash collection is the bane of most small businesses' lives and simultaneously the most important. Poor cash management means you'll struggle to survive. So what can you do to reduce the stress and secure your cash flow? The customer will often leverage any relative strength it has in the knowledge that, while cash is important, you will not wish to upset them.

Experience suggests that the traditional 'incentives' for prompt payment such as interest and threats of litigation tend not to be very successful. Regrettably, the outcome of many commercial disputes is influenced less by the merits of the parties' claims than the depth of their pockets.

So for now, let's assume all else has failed. Your repeated requests for payment have gone unanswered and it's looking likely that this particular account will never be settled. The legal process for debt recovery can be summarised briefly as follows:

Statutory demands

If you are owed less than £750 and your customer is UK-based, the quickest and cheapest form of recovery is to serve a 'statutory demand' on your customer. This gives them 21 days to pay, failing which you will be entitled to go to court for a winding-up (if it is a company) or bankruptcy (if an individual) petition to be served on the customer. The statutory demand takes a standard form and is largely a gap-filling exercise. No one wants to be on the receiving end of one and this tends to flush out quickly the more spurious defences. But be warned: you can only serve a demand where your debt is not disputed by the customer.

Going to court

Pursuing claims through the courts will be time-consuming and expensive. If the amount claimed is less than £10,000 then the claim is a 'small claim' and will go before a County Court as opposed to the High Court (as a rule the County Court tends to be quicker and cheaper). A few points flow from this:

— Even if you're successful, you will not automatically recover all your costs of bringing the action and costs can spiral very quickly in litigation claims. However, where the claim is between £10,000 and £35,000 and you're successful you should stand to recover around 70 per cent of your costs – if you have followed Court procedures (or 'protocol').

— Once you have started the process it is difficult to stop it unilaterally without the risk of an order for costs being made against you.

— It can take eight to twelve months to get to court and you will have to devote a considerable amount of management time to the process.

— The outcome is seldom certain so you should be very clear about the merits of your claim before starting.

— In short, litigation is expensive, time-consuming, risky, and depending on the size of claim there will usually be an element of irrecoverable costs. So do ask yourself, 'Am I throwing good money after bad?'

Protecting against non-payment

It's far better to protect yourself as much as possible against the risk of non-payment in the first place. Try and do the following:

— **Carry out a credit check** against new customers, particularly where the contract is for a significant amount – this will give you an indication of the customer's history and whether there are previous judgements against them for non-payment.

— **Limit your exposure** by taking payments up-front or at regular intervals.

— **Insist on staged payments** against agreed objectives and don't proceed unless you've been paid.

— **Include interest for late payment** in your contract.

— **Make sure your contract is clear** on what you agreed to do and when payment is due.

— **Maintain good lines of communication** with your customers.

— **Put in place efficient credit control procedures.** This is probably the most important tip: keep on top of payment proposals and prevent delays becoming disputes.

By way of illustration, here's an extract from the diary of a small-business owner with efficient cash collection procedures:

Day 7
Called customer as payment was due a week ago. They've received our invoice and are happy with the product. Sent email to confirm conversation.

Day 14
Called customer as gentle reminder that payment not yet received and checking everything OK. Was told that there's no problem and payment is awaiting authorisation.

Day 21
Called customer expressing surprise – they say they're happy with what we did but haven't paid us – and disappointment – they told us payment was on its way. Made them feel embarrassed actually. Payments are processed in one run at month end apparently.

Day 28
Chased customer and explained that we could not understand delay. Clear that they accept we have performed our part of the deal and that we're owed the money. Told them we don't want to escalate this, etc.

Day 35
Payment received.

The moral of the story is to adopt good credit control systems, establish good lines of communication at the right level with your customers narrowing the scope for dispute, and make yourself a (friendly) nuisance.

Sub-contracting

It may be that a particular contract involves skills which are not within your expertise or capacity, in which case you might engage a third party or 'sub-contractor' to perform the relevant functions on your behalf. This is quite common in the construction industry, for instance, where a developer might engage a number of different organisations from architects to bricklayers for a contract it has entered into.

The important thing to remember is that when you engage a sub-contractor you will remain responsible for their mistakes. For that reason you should ensure that your sub-contractor is required to protect you against any claims you suffer which relate to their performance and that they are adequately insured.

Suppliers

While all the issues covered above under 'Customers' are no less important when dealing with suppliers, it is fair to say that in the vast majority of cases when you're buying you will have less ability to control the process. Certainly when dealing with utilities and large corporates (software providers and the like) the idea of engaging in contract negotiations is both unrealistic and, frankly, undesirable. There is little point wasting your time, energy and money on conversations which will only ever have one ending – and it won't be written by you.

But this is definitely not the case where the purchase is a bespoke or significant one-off order – perhaps a new website. In those situations the likelihood is that your bargaining position is stronger and you should try to ensure that any key commercial matters are covered.

These might typically include:

— A clear brief setting out what you expect from your supplier and describing the product as precisely as possible.

— Whether any period should be allowed for ensuring that the product does what it is intended to (and holding back all or part payment until you are satisfied).

— Getting assurances (warranties) from the supplier about the condition, functionality or durability, etc., of the product and spelling out the supplier's obligations if there turns out to be a problem (particularly if you are giving similar assurances to your customer).

— The price (what is included in it) and payment terms.

It would be wise to engage a lawyer to draw up a template of standard purchase conditions for you which are sufficiently broad to allow you to adapt them to different circumstances.

Routes to Market

In terms of selling your product and reaching your potential customers there are a number of avenues, from online trading to engaging a sales agent. There is much to be said for getting others to do the hard work of finding buyers for your product and assuming the risks which go with selling it. This becomes increasingly relevant where you are considering selling overseas.

Beyond direct sales that you may choose to make in person (e.g. your shop) or through your website, your options are essentially:

— Appointing a distributor.
— Appointing an agent.
— Licensing a third party to manufacture or sell your product.

These are very different arrangements in terms of their legal and commercial effect.

Distributor

A distribution arrangement involves you selling your product to the distributor, who then sells the product to third parties – generally retailers. So the distributor is both a buyer and re-seller of your product. The distributor will apply a margin to cover their costs and, as a result of the increased risk and responsibility which it assumes, this will usually be higher than the commission you'd expect to pay to an agent.

The absence of a direct contract between you and the ultimate buyer of your product does not mean that you can avoid any liability completely, but placing a distributor in the supply chain will reduce your exposure – and they, not you, will be chasing up any unpaid invoices.

Agent

In contrast, an agent will identify potential customers for you. Depending upon the terms you agree, the agent can either be authorised to enter into agreements with the customer on your behalf or alternatively act as a middle-man so that the customers purchase your product direct from you. Agents are paid a commission on the sales they introduce.

Distributor vs Agent

The dynamics between you as seller and a distributor on the one hand and an agent on the other are very different:

— You can pass to your distributor a larger degree of your risk.

— Appointing a distributor means less admin as you only need to manage one relationship.

— No compensation should be payable to a distributor on termination of the distribution agreement. Agents, on the other hand, may be entitled to compensation on termination of their agreement under EU regulations.

— You will enjoy less control over a distributor than an agent – this may be problematic where your brand is key and customer satisfaction and pricing are sensitive.

Licensee

Alternatively, you might decide that there is more fun and less stress to be had by licensing someone else to do the heavy lifting of manufacturing and selling your product. If so, any licence agreement should factor in royalties payable to you (e.g. whether there is an up-front fee as well as further agreed revenue-linked royalties), as well as quality control and intellectual property protections, which will be important for your brand.

Whatever your choice of route, take steps to check the credentials of any potential commercial partner and make sure that they are not just reliable but have the

resources and connections to make a success of
your appointment.

Summary

It is in your dealings with suppliers and customers that
your business will be most at risk. This is where you can
find yourself incurring a liability you can't afford or unable
to collect cash owed to you. These dealings are the essence
of your business. Organising them well will help avoid
disputes and wasted time.

So to recap, remember the following:

— Where you are selling, make sure you are in control:
that you dictate when your contract comes into being
and that your terms apply.

— Make sure there is clarity about your contractual
obligations and when you can invoice and be paid.

— Communicate regularly with your customer at the
point of invoicing and flush out any disputes early;
keep on top of credit control; avoid legal action unless
absolutely necessary.

— When you're buying, ask yourself: How important is
the contract to the supplier? What is your bargaining
position? If it's strong, then be clear about what you
expect your supplier to do, what is included in the
price you are paying, and what your rights are if
things go wrong.

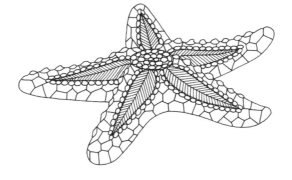

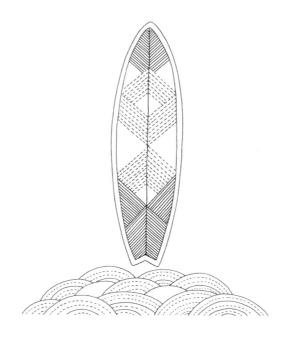

6
E-commerce and Social Media

Regardless of what your business actually is, the chances are that you will have a website and even be trading online. So we're going to take a look at the legal aspects of electronic commerce (e-commerce): selling your products or services via the internet. In particular we will look at the legal and regulatory framework of e-commerce and what steps you should take to ensure your business is compliant.

We will also look at the use of social media in your business and the related risks and legal issues in this area.

Before we get started, a couple of things to note. First, in selling your product online you are creating a contract with your customer in exactly the same way as if they buy your product in person. In the previous chapter we dealt with the concept of contracts and the same basic rules apply to online as to offline trading. It will be vital that your website sets out clearly the process by which the contract between you and your customer comes into being and the terms of that contract.

Second, while our focus here is on the legal aspects of online trading, you will need to ensure that you also have the tools in place to deal with the logistical aspects of online trading, e.g. accepting orders, accepting the customer's money, fulfilment and customer service issues (returns and warranty claims).

Background

The growth in the UK of online sales has been huge in the last few years with an ever-increasing amount being spent via mobile devices such as smartphones and tablets. With consumers becoming increasingly 'tech savvy' and mobile technology developing rapidly, shopping patterns continue to evolve. So online is big, growing and both revolutionising the way established businesses operate and creating an entirely new business model for startups.

The attractions of this model are clear: the ability to offer a wider range of products, speed of transaction and cash collection, the ability to control the shopping experience of your customers and build brand loyalty.

The platform on which you trade may be your own website but could just as easily be a third party's website where your products are offered for sale such as a social networking site like Facebook, an auction site such as eBay or an online retailer such as Etsy. Similarly there are different types of online commercial transaction: business to business (B2B), business to consumer (B2C) and peer to peer (P2P). Each of these arrangements is subject to a variety of rules and regulations which we'll look at in a bit more detail.

Regulations

To help you make sense of the complex and extensive regulatory regime surrounding the area of e-commerce, we are going to focus on three principal areas:

— **E-commerce Regulations**, which apply generally to any business involved in selling online.

— **Distance Selling Regulations** – applicable to transactions where you and your customer do not come face to face such as email, phone and in this case online.

— **Privacy Regulations**, which among other things regulate the use of cookies.

Why does all this matter? First, because failure to comply can result in you as the supplier being liable to pay damages to your customer as well as giving them the right to cancel an order and demand a refund. Second, there is the reputational damage to your business that will invariably follow. And finally there is the potential criminal liability which can flow from mis-stating a consumer's legal rights.

E-commerce Regulations

The existing regulations were designed to harmonise e-commerce services across the EU and clarify the rights and obligations of both businesses and consumers. The aspiration was to boost consumer confidence in the new medium while encouraging businesses through a 'light touch' regulatory approach. The regulations have a wide application covering not just businesses that sell online but also those that advertise on the internet or by email. The principal issues with which you need to be familiar are:

Applicable laws

Although the regulations apply a 'country of origin' principle (so that in theory a UK-based business need only comply with UK law), B2C contracts are specifically excluded. Consequently, when dealing with consumers directly you will need to comply with the relevant laws of the country where people can purchase your product. The prudent course is to ensure that your contract is subject to English law while stating that in the case of consumers this won't deprive them of protection provided by the laws of their own country.

Information

You are required to make certain information available on your website at all times. This ranges from including details of the name, address and VAT number of your business to ensuring that any prices on the website are clear and specifying whether tax and delivery costs are included in the purchase price (see also Chapter 8).

Placing the order

Certain information must be provided to the buyer before orders are placed – in other words, before the contract is made. By way of example:

— Your website must provide your customer with the technical means for identifying and correcting errors made in placing an order. So make sure your customer has a clear option to go 'back' before finalising the transaction.

— Orders must be electronically acknowledged without undue delay. Note 'acknowledged' is not the same thing as 'accepted' which may help you avoid becoming bound to sell at an incorrect (lower) cost because of pricing errors on your website.

— Your customer must be able to store and print your terms and conditions.

Spam

Internet advertising and marketing are caught by the E-commerce and Privacy Regulations: 'Commercial communications' must be clearly recognisable and identify the person on whose behalf the communication is made, i.e. your business. These regulations extend to 'spam' (or 'unsolicited commercial communications') and among other things state that:

— They must be identifiable as unsolicited commercial communications from the subject line of the email.

— Where the recipient is an individual you must have their prior consent unless you have previously obtained their details through a sale or negotiation. (A corporate recipient is not subject to the same restrictions so a spam email to the same person at their company email address would not be an infringement.)

Distance Selling Regulations

These regulations apply to a B2C transaction or 'distance contract' where you and your customer do not come face to face. An online transaction is a classic example of this but this category would also include transactions involving email, phone or a catalogue. The effect of the regulations is to give your customer specific rights, namely:

— **To receive clear information** about your business and the goods or services before the contract is concluded and confirmed in writing, e.g. by email
— **To cancel the order** (or contract)
— **To a refund** in certain circumstances

A few points to note:

Information
As the seller you must provide your customer with certain information before the order is placed and accepted. This matters because failure to do so means your contract will be unenforceable against the customer, which would be unfortunate if they haven't paid. The list of information is lengthy and includes such things as a description of the goods, price, delivery and cancellation rights.

Cancellation
Your customer can cancel their order (or contract) during the cancellation or 'cooling off' period (normally seven working days). There are exceptions to this right, e.g. where goods have been made to order.

Refunds
When an order is cancelled the customer must be repaid as soon as possible. This would include the price and any delivery costs paid by the customer.

Performance
As the supplier you are required to fulfil the order within 30 days from the date of it being placed. If this is likely to be a problem then you should agree an alternative delivery date. Failing that you must notify your customer and issue a refund.

Privacy Regulations and cookies

We touched on cookies in Chapter 2. The Privacy Regulations specify that the use of cookies is permitted only if visitors to your site have been provided with clear and comprehensive information about the purpose of the cookie and have given their consent. This means that as a starting-point you need to identify cookies operating on your website, their purpose and the information held. You need to decide what level of detail will be provided to your user and how this will be brought to their attention, perhaps via a link to an 'information about cookies' page. Finally consider how you are going to obtain the user's consent, e.g. will you require them to actively accept?

Trading disclosures

If you trade via a company, your company's full company name, number, registered office and place of registration must be displayed on your website. This doesn't have to be on the homepage and many sites opt to have a separate 'legal' page discreetly housing all this information.

Data Protection Act

In Chapter 2 we also considered the obligations imposed by the DPA on those involved in the 'processing' of personal data. Online transactions will inevitably contain personal data about individuals, e.g. your customer will be required to supply their details for you to fulfil their order. The obligations under the DPA fall on the 'data controller' and, in relation to personal data collected via your website, you as the website operator will be the data controller. The Information Commissioner's Office has published a checklist for small businesses operating online to ensure they collect and use personal data properly (*www.ico.org.uk*).

Compliance

Having identified the key e-commerce regulations, the best way to ensure you have complied with them is to have a comprehensive set of terms and conditions of sale on your website. These serve two critical functions: they govern the contract with your buyer and help you satisfy many of the compliance obligations referred to above. We dealt in Chapter 2 with the sort of things which you should include here. Beware: simply placing them on your website will not suffice. Ideally your website should provide a link to the terms so that it is clear they have been brought to the customer's attention. Here are a few options:

— A link to your website terms accompanied by a statement that use of your website means acceptance of your terms.

— Preventing your customer from proceeding without clicking an 'I accept' button next to a link to your website terms.

— Preventing the visitor from proceeding without clicking an 'I accept' button on your website terms – this is the preferred method.

Finally, be clear on your liabilities and obligations where you are selling to consumers overseas. And ensure that your privacy policy addresses how your website users' data will be collected, used, disclosed and maintained.

Social Media

The advent of new and various media – from blogs to videos and social networks – presents real opportunities for companies to interact with their customers and to develop both their brand and brand loyalty. Its reach and immediacy are simultaneously both the attraction and risk of social media, and the inherent difficulties in imposing effective safeguards mean that its misuse can pose significant risks for your business.

Risks

Whatever your business it is inevitable that you will have some engagement with social media through a variety of means:

Employees

Your staff might use social media for personal or business purposes by using your website or a third party's such as Twitter or Facebook – either context can affect your business. Similarly, through networks such as LinkedIn, employees may disclose confidential information relating to your business, plans or your customers. Content posted by staff (e.g. comments about colleagues) can form the basis of a harassment or defamation claims. Be aware that anti-discrimination laws can hold employers liable for discrimination by their employees.

Third parties

You may find that critical comments about your business or products are posted on third-party blogs or other social media sites which need a swift response or action.

Your website users

Comments posted on your website by visitors to your site might infringe third-party IP or be defamatory.

Aside from any potential financial liability, all of these issues pose potentially serious reputational risks for your business. Not to mention the inevitable loss of productivity which flows from excessive social media usage!

Protections

So what steps should you consider taking to protect your business and minimise the potential for claims?

Your first step should be the adoption of a simple Social Media Policy, which might cover:

— Rules about accessing social media sites during business hours.

— Giving notice of monitoring by you as the employer and how such information will be used.

— Requiring staff to include a disclaimer in any personal blog (that any views are not representative of the employer's views, etc.)

— Reminding staff that unauthorised disclosure of confidential information is prohibited.

Importantly, it should also inform staff that disciplinary action can follow any breach of the policy and you reserve your right to remove offensive content. A word of caution here: the corollary of these restrictions and controls is potential claims by your staff based on, for example, breach of their privacy or freedom of expression.

The key as ever is moderation and making sure that your policies are sensible and appropriate.

Secondly, you should implement practices to monitor business-related use by your staff of third-party social media, networking and blogging on your own website, and comments about your business posted on third-party sites (it's always worth keeping an eye on what is being said about you!) Put in place website terms of use and privacy policies, and train your staff in online behaviour. In addition, check your staff employment contracts to ensure that unauthorised disclosure of confidential information is explicitly prohibited.

While this might all sound a bit much, the objective is to ensure that damaging posts, blogs, tweets and the like are brought to your attention as soon as possible, giving you the opportunity to take appropriate action. Social media is subject to the same legal rules as comments or information published in any other form, so your rights could be based in defamation, infringement of your IP, or perhaps the improper release of confidential information.

The action you take will depend on the circumstances but could include requesting that a post on a third-party website be taken down, the issue of a correction and apology, the deletion of posts on your website, posting a correction or reply (perhaps using your blog or a video posting), or in extreme cases taking legal proceedings. However, a variety of factors from the anonymity of the web to the expense of litigation and the inevitable further unwanted publicity make legal action very much a last resort.

Summary

So to draw some conclusions. **Online trading** is a huge and growing medium. It is also heavily regulated and contains significant traps for the unwary. Getting it wrong can have both financial and reputational repercussions. Having identified your potential exposure, the key is to establish that, as far as practical, you have policies and procedures in place which will provide a defence to any claims against your business, reduce your exposure or at the very least reduce your liability.

Used properly, **social media** should be an integral part of your company's communications strategy. The key for any business, startup or otherwise, is to ensure a clear understanding between founders and team members of its use in relation to the business; and implement policies to minimise the risks to your business inherent in its improper use.

7
Building Your Team

For many entrepreneurs, starting out can be a solitary
and scary experience. Whether you are a sole trader
or in partnership with a couple of colleagues, it is
unlikely that you will start your business with a strong
supporting cast to whom you can turn. One of the
tricks to being a successful startup is not only to
recognise your limitations, but to pick and retain
the right people.

In this chapter we are going to focus on a few of the legal
aspects in the team-building process across the various
stages, from hiring and firing to incentivising and managing.
    A word of caution: this area, like many others covered
in *Do Protect*, is highly regulated. There is insufficient
space to cover all aspects of employment law here but,
as ever, the intention is to highlight the bigger issues and
provide some guidance.

Types of Employment Relationship

Over the last decade or so, working patterns and practices
in the UK have become increasingly diverse as both
employers and workers seek greater flexibility.

So when it comes to recruiting it is important to understand the basis on which you engage any individual as their employment status (employee, freelancer and so on) will not only affect the rights they acquire but also their tax, national insurance and pensions arrangements. It is important that the employee's status reflects the reality of the working relationship as this is what will be considered if there is any legal challenge to it. In essence there are three types of relationship:

Employee

These are the essential characteristics of an employee: he or she is engaged to perform their work personally; you as employer provide the work and the employee is required to do it; you provide the 'tools' to do the job and control what, how and when they do it. There can still be a lot of flexibility to an employment relationship such as working part time, on a casual basis, temporary or fixed term contracts. Directors and shareholders of companies as well as members of LLPs can also be employees if they are working for the business.

The significance is that employee status automatically confers a number of rights on the individual: some are immediate, and others are acquired with service – as we'll see in the course of this chapter.

Self-employed / freelance

Alternatively you might engage an individual on a self-employed basis, such as contractor or consultant. A genuinely self-employed consultant will have far fewer rights than an employee but the trade-off is that the business will have far less control over the individual.

Using contractors or outsourcing work can be useful where services are needed on an ad hoc basis such as book keeping, design projects, human resources or IT. Self-employed individuals should raise invoices for their services.

Agency workers

A further option is to use workers provided by an agency. The 'temp' will be the agency's employee and so the individual's rights as regards your business are very limited. Agency workers are entitled to the same pay and basic working conditions as your equivalent permanent staff after 12 weeks' engagement.

It is important to remember that certain rights apply whatever the nature of the working relationship so for instance the anti-discrimination legislation applies to employees, self-employed and agency staff as well as job applicants. Similarly, the National Minimum Wage (NMW) applies to all types of work with the exception of the genuinely self-employed and directors who are not also employees.

In summary, the law for employers can be complex territory and you would do well to run any arrangement past your lawyer particularly if you are assuming that the recruit will not be an employee!

Interns

Finally a few words on interns whose use has flourished as economic conditions tightened. There is no agreed definition or legal status for 'intern' but generally it is taken to mean someone who is gaining work experience.

You need to be very careful in deciding whether to take on interns and what they do, as they can be entitled to NMW if they are a 'worker'. In deciding whether NMW applies, a court will look at what the intern actually does and not necessarily what has been agreed. If they are required to turn up to work and you provide work for them (however minor) then they will be entitled to NMW from the outset. In addition, if they are rewarded for any work beyond genuine out of pocket expenses they can be classed as a worker. Depending on the working arrangements an intern who qualifies for NMW will gain statutory rights as an employee or a freelancer (explained above). HMRC is taking a strict view on the use of unpaid interns and so it is likely to be very difficult for you as an employer to show that it was genuinely voluntary work experience and that NMW does not apply.

As things stand volunteers, students undertaking work placements of less than a year as part of their higher or further education programme and school work placements do not qualify for NMW.

Apprenticeships are an alternative arrangement for providing meaningful work experience and gaining a willing worker. They can include professional skills as well as more traditional trades. An apprenticeship is usually for a fixed term or until a level of qualification is achieved. They are still studying and so will not be working full time. The NMW for recognised apprenticeships is set at a lower rate than for other categories of worker.

Hiring

When hiring there a number of matters to consider, not merely to maximise your chances of finding the best candidate, but also to minimise potential claims from disappointed applicants so do tread carefully at each stage.

Process

Let's start with the dangers of discrimination. From the very beginning of the recruitment process the anti-discrimination legislation should be borne in mind. The context for this is the Equality Act 2010 which prohibits discrimination, harassment and victimisation in recruitment or employment because of a specific 'protected characteristic' – namely age, disability, religion/ belief, marriage/ civil partnership, pregnancy and maternity, race, gender reassignment, sex and sexual orientation.

'Discrimination' is treating an individual less favourably because of such a 'protected characteristic' than a person without that characteristic – e.g. refusing to interview a candidate because of their sex. Unfortunately discrimination can also occur indirectly. For example, a requirement to work full time could mean that women are placed at a disadvantage compared to men, as women tend to bear childcare responsibilities and so working full time may not be an option. Ultimately it would be up to you as the employer to justify the condition, e.g. in this case the requirement that the post is filled on a full time basis.

One further point: Where an individual has a disability there is a duty on employers to make 'reasonable adjustments'. You should ask applicants to identify any disability and whether they require any adjustments.

These can include physical changes to the place where you will hold the interview and to arrangements for the interview itself, such as the time it is held. Unhelpfully perhaps, what is 'reasonable' will depend on each individual situation.

Position

Having identified the need to recruit you should draw up a detailed job description. Identifying the type of role you are filling will also help you focus on the experience, qualifications and qualities you are looking for in the individual. Consider carefully the genuine requirements for the role and if any of these could create a barrier for a potential candidate. Ask yourself, can the requirement be justified? For example, does the role need to be full time? Can it be school hours or flexi time? Would you consider a job share?

Adverts

Take care that advertisements avoid any potential discrimination and beware the use of social media to vet candidates – this can be risky particularly if you obtain information about a protected characteristic and the candidate claims your decision was based on that.

Candidate selection

How are you going to select the best candidate? You may need to draw up a shortlist of those most suitable by comparing their details against the job requirements. While it is usual to interview the potential recruit, you may consider conducting a separate skills test.

Interview

Consider who will conduct the interview and establish your selection criteria early. Make sure there is consistency in your questions. Once again, take care to ensure that your interview process doesn't give grounds for a discrimination complaint – questions should be relevant to the requirements of the job and you should avoid asking irrelevant questions relating to 'protected characteristics' – plans for children, for example.

Keep a record of the interview; applicants will have the right to access their information under the DPA, which would include the interview process. So care needs to be taken in making any notes or comments about candidates. If a rejected candidate asks for feedback, be prepared to provide it.

Offer

Any offer of employment should be in writing, specifying any conditions which need to be met and marked 'subject to contract'. In terms of possible conditions the most important requirement is that the individual can prove they are eligible to work in the relevant country as there are substantial penalties for employers who get this wrong! Other usual conditions include satisfactory references (you should approach these only after acceptance of the offer), proof of qualifications held, confirmation that there are no contractual restrictions which might affect the candidate's ability to fulfil the role, and for some positions a clear criminal record check. Some employers also undertake a medical check, but this should only be required after seeking advice.

Your letter should also warn the candidate against

resigning from any existing position until these conditions are satisfied. Lastly, set a deadline for acceptance.

Contract

Good practice is to issue an employment contract as soon as possible. This doesn't have to be too formal and can take the form of a letter. In any event you must provide (section 1 of the Employment Rights Act 1996) basic particulars of employment in writing within eight weeks of their start date.

Start

There are a number of administrative requirements which are typically dealt with from obtaining the individual's P45, completion of appropriate internal forms, confirmation of how any probation period is to work and a formal induction. The induction process should cover:

— **Staff procedures**, e.g. holiday requests and pay arrangements
— **Health & Safety** (location of fire exits, etc.) and working practices
— **Introduction to the business**, e.g. products/services, key customers, plans, etc.

Confidential Information

During their employment an employee is likely to acquire confidential information about your business, develop business contacts or devise new products – all at your expense. Clearly if they leave and use this information in competition with you it could seriously harm your business. So how to protect yourself? For senior employees, it is important to include in their contract provisions dealing with confidential information – defining what it is and restricting its use – and intellectual property to ensure that anything created during the employment belongs to you.

The contract can also include restrictions that apply to the employee after their employment has ended. Suitably drafted restrictions can legitimately prevent the employee from competing with you for a limited period of time. While Courts dislike these sort of provisions seeing them as restraint of trade, restrictions that have been upheld include preventing an employee from:

— competing within a defined geographic area
— soliciting or dealing with customers or prospective customers over whom they have influence
— poaching staff from your business

Similar restrictions should also be used for consultants with access to equally sensitive information.

A few general words of caution on restrictions: first, given the antipathy of the Courts towards them, restrictions should be tailored for the individual situation to maximise their chances of enforceability; and second, they are only suitable for more senior positions.

Termination

If you find yourself in the regrettable position of having to terminate an employee's employment it is vital that you understand the individual's rights. If the process is not handled properly you could give the employee a claim which will be difficult to defend.

The anti-discrimination legislation referred to earlier also applies to dismissals so it is important to ensure there is no potentially discriminatory reason for the decision. By way of example, redundancy dismissals based on length of service (last in first out, etc.) can amount to age discrimination as younger employees will be at a disadvantage – on the whole they are more likely to have shorter service.

Other than in cases of gross misconduct employees are entitled to receive their notice or payment in lieu of notice. Failure to pay this can lead to a claim for wrongful dismissal. The minimum statutory entitlement is one week's pay for each complete year of service up to a maximum of 12 weeks.

An employee may also be able to claim unfair dismissal. In the first two years of their employment any claim is restricted to a dismissal on limited specified grounds (such as whistleblowing or reasons connected to pregnancy) but thereafter the burden shifts and for a dismissal to be fair it must be for one of five reasons:

— **conduct** (e.g. an act of serious misconduct)
— **illegality** (where continuing to employ the employee would contravene the law, e.g. in breach of immigration rules)
— **redundancy** (e.g. a business downturn requiring you to reduce headcount)
— **capability** (this can include poor performance and ill-health)
— **'some other substantial reason'** (a catch-all category)

Once the reason has been identified you as the employer must still act reasonably and follow a fair procedure appropriate to the circumstances. Instant dismissal should be avoided. Even if the employee is caught red handed, they should still be given an opportunity to offer an explanation.

Compensation for a successful claim can be substantial but irrespective of the success of any claim you can incur significant management time and legal costs in defending a claim which will usually not be recoverable.

Staff Incentives

Implementing schemes to motivate your employees can have obvious benefits for your business. First and foremost, you want those people you have carefully hired and spent time training to stay.

There are a number of arrangements available to you as an employer, from the straight cash bonus linked to sales or profits, to share schemes and even 'phantom' share schemes (where the employee receives a cash award linked to the value of your business). There may be tax implications both for your business and your employee in these arrangements and it is always sensible to discuss your proposals with your accountants or tax advisers first.

While few business owners readily embrace the concept, my experience suggests that there can be significant commercial benefits to a business in bringing employees into the equity base. The complications of sharing equity are more than offset by the positive impact ownership can have on your staff.

It is worth mentioning the new concept of employee-shareholder which has been introduced and allows employees and new recruits to give up certain statutory employment rights (including the right to claim for unfair dismissal and the right to a statutory redundancy payment) in return for shares in their employer.

Possible share schemes range from those that are tax-favoured (where you have obtained approval from HMRC) and a variety of other share incentive plans that do not confer any tax advantages for the employee. Structured correctly the tax advantages for the employee can include paying no income tax on the grant or exercise of the share option and, depending on the size of the interest and period of ownership, tax relief on the disposal of the shares. The tax-approved schemes include:

— Company share option plans
— Savings-related share option schemes
— Share incentive plans – where the employee can acquire shares rather than share options
— Enterprise management incentive options

To find out more about these schemes, a good starting point is the UK government's own website (*www.hmrc.gov.uk*). Predictably, there are a number of technical issues to consider when implementing an incentive scheme. There are also commercial factors, such as deciding when the incentive will 'vest' (i.e. when the real value of the arrangement crystallises in the employee's hands) and what happens if the employee leaves your organisation while holding shares or with an option to acquire them. All these matters can be dealt with in well-drafted documentation so that you, as employer, can have comfort in the knowledge that an employee who leaves your business won't benefit from the efforts of those left behind or have the potential to derail a future sale of your business.

Finally a brief word on pensions. Under recent regulations all businesses will have to automatically enrol eligible workers into a pension scheme and make contributions to it unless the employee opts out. Implementation is staggered; startups and smaller businesses will be required to comply by 2017.

Summary

Finding and retaining the right team will be crucial to the success of your business. This is a notoriously complex and sophisticated area for new businesses but the principal points can be distilled to a few key objectives:

— Reduce your business risk when taking on or dismissing staff.
— Protect your business with thorough employment contracts.
— Where possible, align your staff's interests with those of your business.

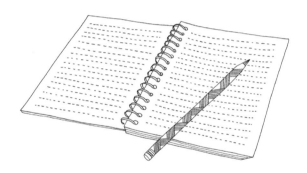

8
Essential Admin

One of the most common complaints from those starting their own business is the level of admin and paperwork they have to deal with. These obligations will vary depending on whether you are operating as a sole trader, in partnership or through a limited company (as outlined in Chapter 1).

Like the rest of this book this chapter is concerned with administrative obligations on businesses operating in the UK. Be mindful that different obligations will apply in other jurisdictions.

In addition, as every business needs a place in which to operate so we'll also look briefly at commercial property.

Accounting

Regardless of your business structure, you will have some dealings with the taxman and high on your action list should be the appointment of an accountant who will be able to guide you through your accounting and tax obligations. With that caveat, here's an overview of the different accounting obligations of the various business structures.

Companies

Accounting records

All companies, regardless of size, must keep – in hard or electronic form – accounting records of sums received and spent, as well as details of their assets and liabilities. These records are available for inspection by the company's directors and secretary – but not its shareholders.

Accounts

The directors of every company must prepare accounts for each financial year. A financial year can be any period up to 18 months (except for your first one, which can't be less than 6 months) but is typically 12 months. You can choose the end date (the 'accounting reference date'). This could be 31 December – so your financial year would start neatly on 1 January – but the choice is yours.

Filing

Your accounts must be filed with Companies House within nine months of the end of each financial year. A copy of the accounts and reports must be sent to shareholders, though it is permissible instead to upload them to the company's website. Failure to deliver accounts to Companies House on time is a criminal offence and incurs a penalty, though there is a procedure for applying for an extension.

Tax

You will remember from Chapter 1 that your company is a separate legal entity and as such will need to complete an appropriate tax return to the tax authority. It will be liable to corporation tax on the profits it makes in the year. Separately, as an employee you will be liable to income tax on your earnings and any income from your business.

Typically the company will deduct this from your remuneration and account to the taxman for it on your behalf. In addition, if the business pays you a dividend as a shareholder out of its taxed profits, you will be liable to income tax on that dividend.

As we noted in the first chapter, the company structure is not renowned for its tax efficiency …

Small companies

Most startups will qualify as a 'small company', being a company which ticks two of the following: annual turnover of less than £6.5m, total assets of less than £3.26m, and/or average number of employees is less than 50. While you will still be required to prepare standard accounts and reports (a profit and loss account, a full balance sheet, a directors' report and an auditor's report), for a small company it's actually only the balance sheet which needs to be filed with Companies House and this can be done in an abbreviated form.

Accounts can be filed online and as a small company you can claim exemption from the obligation for accounts to be audited. However, there are a few conditions to be observed and a copy of the company's full accounts must still be sent to any shareholders you have.

Limited Liability Partnerships

LLPs are subject to a separate accounting regime within the Companies Act; however, the duties to keep accounting records, preparation and filing of accounts and exemptions and concessions for 'small LLPs' are similar to those for companies.

Partnerships and sole traders

There are very few accounting requirements for partnerships and sole traders – and no filings to be made with Companies House – but appropriate tax returns will still need to be made to HMRC.

In the case of a partnership, a tax return is made on behalf of all the partners showing any profits. Each individual partner is then subject to income tax on their share under the self-assessment rules – each partner is solely responsible for the tax due on their share. A partner is taxed under a different regime to an employee of a company.

As a sole trader you will be liable to income tax on your business's profits and a tax return must be made to HMRC under the self-assessment procedures.

Banking

Your business will need to open a bank account. It is important to remember that whether or not you choose to run your business through a separate entity such as a company, you should keep your business's banking arrangements separate from your own. Not least, this will help to ensure that accounting records and book-keeping is cleaner and avoid any confusion with business expenses being paid out of your personal account and vice versa.

If the bank is not providing your business with any funding then the formalities should be (relatively) straightforward and there will be no need to provide any form of collateral for the bank. That said, the bank will have compliance procedures to follow and when opening the account you will need to produce personal identification as well as details of your business.

A key matter to establish is the signatories to your mandate – a standard form of instruction to the bank with details of the signatures and names of those individuals authorised to sign cheques on behalf of the business – and any limit for each signatory. Often these will be one or more company directors or partners with the number of required signatures increasing in line with the amount of the cheque being signed.

Insurance

In the scheme of things this is a topic which is commonly at the bottom of the to-do list. Yet ironically it should be one of the first things a startup considers. Depending on the nature of your business, it may be that customers (particularly larger corporates and public sector bodies) will require you to have appropriate levels of insurance in place before engaging you. By way of illustration, self-employed professionals giving advice in the areas of law or accountancy are required to have professional indemnity insurance in place covering them for negligence.

Irrespective of the nature of your business, there are a few types of insurance that are likely to be relevant:

— **Public liability:** protects against potential accidents involving third parties while on your premises.

— **Employers' liability:** protects your business against claims by employees. Subject to some exceptions, such as sole traders, this insurance is a legal requirement where you employ staff – even if only on a part-time basis – and requires a minimum cover of £5m.

— **Directors' and officers' liability** (D&O insurance): insurance taken out by companies to enable them to indemnify their directors against any financial loss they may incur in the course of their duties. It is not a legal requirement.

— **Trade credit:** enables your business to protect itself against non-payment by your customers in certain circumstances. Where you are exporting your products, the UK government's Export Credit Guarantee Department should be a port of call (*www.ukexportfinance.gov.uk*).

— **Business interruption:** where your business is closed because of acts beyond your control.

Depending upon the nature of your business there are other bespoke insurances which it would be prudent to consider, e.g. property, environmental and construction insurance. And you shouldn't forget personal insurance, which you should take out to protect yourself against being prevented from being able to work due to illness, for example.

It will come as little surprise that insurance does not come cheap and, as ever, it is worth shopping around. Finally, make sure that you are not paying for more cover than you need.

VAT

Value added tax (VAT) has been with us in the UK since 1973 when we joined the EEC. It is a frighteningly complex area subject to lengthy European and UK legislation, directives and regulations.

The tax is charged on any supply of goods or services made in the UK where the supply is made by a taxable person (see below). While in principle VAT is borne by your customer, it is you – as the supplier – who are required to account for it to HMRC. In practice the regime operates by you deducting the VAT chargeable on the things you buy for your business from other businesses ('input tax') from the VAT you charge on your sales ('output tax'). You account to HMRC for the difference.

> **Remember:** the VAT return is entirely separate from the tax returns mentioned earlier that you and your business will need to file in respect of your trading activities during the year.

For VAT purposes supplies you make are divided into taxable and exempt. There are three categories of taxable supplies:

— **Standard rate:** 20 per cent at the time of writing – most items are standard-rated.
— **Reduced rate:** 5 per cent on a limited number of items, e.g. domestic fuel.
— **Zero rate:** food, children's clothes, books and newspapers fall into this category.

Exempt supplies relate to matters such as education, insurance and health – dentists, for example.

A 'taxable person' is an individual, limited company or other entity that is registered or required to be registered for VAT. You are required to be registered where either your taxable products or services in the previous 12 months exceed the threshold for registration (£79,000 from 1 April 2013) or you expect to exceed that threshold in the next 30 days.

That being said, there are advantages to registration, for example if your VAT-able purchases exceed your VAT-able supplies, HMRC will reimburse you the difference, and registration can provide security and kudos with your customers.

You will have to keep records for all your VAT purchases and supplies and typically will complete a return to HMRC quarterly. This can be done online and in fact now has to be when you start paying VAT or when your turnover exceeds £100,000. Your net VAT payment is made at the same time.

Some good news: if you take advantage of the Annual Accounting Scheme (your anticipated turnover must be less than £1.35m), then you only have to fill out one return per year and you can pay VAT in nine instalments with a balancing payment at the end of the year. The scheme is intended to reduce your paperwork and ease your cash flow.

Trading Disclosures

Businesses have to comply with regulations concerning those places where it must display its name and details:

Company

Your company's registered name must be displayed at the following places: its registered office (this won't necessarily be your place of work but perhaps your accountant's address); the place(s) of work for you and the business; on cheques (as a director you will be personally liable on any cheque which doesn't comply); on invoices (additional information will be needed on a VAT invoice); and on receipts. In addition, your company's business letters, orders and, as we've seen previously, your website must display the following details: your company's registered name; the part of the UK in which it is registered (England and Wales, Scotland, etc.); and its registered number and registered office.

Your company and its directors are liable to a fine for failure to comply with these obligations.

LLPs

Essentially the same rules apply for LLPs. In addition, any business correspondence must contain either all of the members' names or not refer to any of them.

Sole trader/partnership

Your name and/or the name of each partner, and an address where official or legal communications (such as writs) can be sent, must be displayed on business letters, orders, invoices and receipts, demands for payment and your business premises. This address can be your trading address.

Premises

As a rule of thumb the best advice for any startup when it comes to premises is, if at all possible, avoid commitment. Depending on the size and nature of your business (i.e. your requirements in terms of equipment, machinery, staff and so on), operating from home or a shared office can be the ideal solution. It is also worth considering how important location is to you. Do you need a city centre presence if much of your business is going to be done online?

If you are to take space then the likelihood is that you will rent it. Negotiations with landlords have historically followed a predictable path and usually ending badly for the tenant. However, the Code for Leasing Business Premises in England and Wales 2007 was intended to redress the balance and achieve a fairer deal for commercial tenants by, among other things, providing them with information to negotiate the best deal. A few words of caution: the code is voluntary – not all landlords will choose to offer leases which comply with the code, but you should ask your landlord whether theirs does – and there is no substitute for professional advice. By way of a pointer, bear the following in mind when considering your lease:

— How long is it and do you have the right to end it early or the right to extend it? Flexibility is key for a new business and accepting a fixed term of more than five years should be avoided.

— What's the rent and when will it be reviewed? What is included in the rent? Is a rent deposit required and if so where will it be held? (Depending on your bargaining position you would do well to avoid paying one.)

— What are your obligations in terms of repairs to the premises and who is responsible for insurance?

— Do you have an obligation to leave the premises as you find them (aka a 'dilapidations' obligation)? If so, take photos of the internal and external condition of the premises at the outset to avoid arguments later about how the property looked when you took occupation.

— If your business is a company then you will almost invariably be asked to provide a personal guarantee – which as we noted earlier you would be well advised to resist.

— Last but not least, be clear about any potential stamp duty (tax) liability you might have to pay.

The moral of the story is to avoid commitment if you can. If you have to commit to a lease then avoid giving any personal guarantee for the rent and negotiate flexibility in terms of your ability to walk away.

Summary

There's no escaping the fact that this is a dry topic. But to remind you of the Introduction to this book, the importance of attention to detail cannot be under-estimated. This is the detail.

There are a number of administrative challenges a new business faces, from negotiations with a landlord to opening a bank account and from VAT registration to insurance. These are time-consuming and potentially complicated activities, but are part of the essential foundations of your business.

Organisation is key. When it comes to compliance there is no substitute for engaging advisers who can take away some of this burden and free you up to get on with the business of generating profit and cash. The cash spent outsourcing these administrative functions can often be less than the value of the lost management time and business opportunities involved in doing it yourself.

9
Selling Your Business

For many entrepreneurs, the idea of exiting their business may seem irrelevant. It's simply not part of the plan. For others, this may be the primary reason for going into business in the first place: to build up their assets, then sell up.

Whatever the incentive or motivation for deciding to sell, the process frequently follows a less than direct path. It is vital to have experienced advisers on your team who know how to guide you through the process while keeping any disruption to your business to a minimum.

While we are looking at the legal aspects of the business sale process, most accountants will cheerily tell you that this is only part – and a minor one – of the overall scheme. Lawyers are invariably the last ones to the party and by then the accountants will have invested time and costs in helping to identify potential buyers and managing the process. It is fair to say that we are focusing here on the 'business end' of matters but it is in this detail that hard cash can be won and lost.

Process

The conventional process of selling your business involves a number of stages and protagonists; handling these efficiently and effectively will be key to your outcome. Let's take them in turn.

Sale processes

The time has come when you want or need to sell your business, so how do you go about it? We'll come to finding your buyer, but in terms of the process there are essentially two ways in which you might exit your business:

— a sale to a buyer who approaches you or alternatively is approached by you – 'off-market' as it's known.
— a sale to a buyer who is the last man standing following a competitive marketing or 'auction' of your business.

The off-market sale is by some distance the more common and certainly more straightforward. As for the auction process, it's primary advantage is the competitive tension it creates between interested parties which, in theory, drives up your price. Although the auction process is synonymous with the sale of larger businesses this is not exclusively the case, but there must be sufficient interest in your business. An auction needs careful management and you should engage advisers (accountants, corporate finance advisers, lawyers) who have a proven track record in this field.

Sale structures

In terms of the legal process, there are essentially two methods of selling your business, depending upon its structure. If your business is a company, then you can either personally sell your shares, which is known as a share sale, or your company can sell its assets and distribute the cash it receives to you as a shareholder/ member, known as an assets sale.

The comparative complexities of the ownership structure of an LLP mean that any sale of its underlying business will invariably take the form of the LLP itself selling its assets.

If you are a sole trader or partnership then as the owner of those assets you will sell them directly to your buyer.

For a company the implications of these two structures can be summarised as follows:

	Share Sale	Assets Sale
Who's the seller?	Shareholders of your company	Your company
What's being sold?	Issued shares of your company	Your company's business and assets
Legal effect	Change of ownership of your company (no effect on company's assets)	Your company's assets are transferred. No change of ownership of your company

The most appropriate route invariably depends on the circumstances though most lawyers will tell you that a share sale is cleaner as the transfer of a collection of individual assets from land to trademarks can be messy. However, the reality is that tax considerations commonly drive the deal structure.

Partial exits

This chapter deals primarily with the sale of your entire business. However, there is an alternative scenario where you as the owner may decide to retain an interest in your business and instead realise part of your investment. For many owner-managers the issue of selling their business is less about money than the prospect of walking away from something they have built up over many years. The emotional aspects of selling your business should never be underestimated and it is for this reason that some transactions are structured to leave the owner with a legacy shareholding in their business.

It is worth pointing out that a partial exit can also be the creation of the buyer, who may use the structure as a means of deferring payment, incentivising you as the owner, resolving differences over valuation or simply by way of a 'wait-and-see' approach to buying your business.

These arrangements, and the size of any retained stake, will also be influenced by the owner's appetite for continued involvement, which will be complicated by the fact that they will no longer be in control of the business. If there is to be such a deal then as owner you should focus on:

— Defining a clear role for you in the business.
— The amount of time you will have to devote.
— A specific time frame – as a rule, the shorter the better.
— Any restrictions on your pursuit of other interests.
— Terms for the purchase of your remaining interest – the reality is that the only buyers will be the other shareholders.

Partial exits are a useful way for an owner to 'de-risk' their investment in the business but such arrangements can be messy and need careful consideration.

Value, Price and Payment

For good or bad the value (or worth) of your business does not necessarily equate to the price you get. As we will see there are a variety of factors which influence price while valuation tends to be highly subjective. In addition, how and when you get paid is of course key. A few words on these aspects:

Value

So, what's your business worth? A pragmatist will tell you unhelpfully that it's worth exactly what someone is willing to pay. However, you have to start somewhere and there are some excellent textbooks explaining the wonders of discounted cash flows, net assets and multiples of profits as a means of valuing your business, which if nothing else give you an idea of where to start. Valuation is very much an art rather than a science and it is surprising how often the price is disconnected from the underlying numbers, e.g. where a trade competitor pays a premium reflecting the strategic benefit of your business to their own. The recent $19bn acquisition by Facebook of What's App (a business with relatively small revenue and which has yet to generate $1 of profit) provides a good example of a strategic premium – in this case to enable Facebook to access a particular messaging market.

Price

If valuation is where you start, then price is where you end. The price may be fixed (i.e. unconditional – the ideal scenario for you), but is commonly set by reference to factors such as the value of your business's assets at the point of sale, or 'completion', or even future profits, and adjusted accordingly. It is in part in the negotiation of these rules around the calculation and payment of the price that your advisers earn their corn – and yours. Bottom line: keep the structure as simple as possible with as few conditions as you can negotiate.

Payment

Ideally you will be paid in full and in cash on signing. In reality, the buyer will seek to protect themselves by delaying full payment until the price adjustments are completed or a period (usually a year) has elapsed during which there have been no surprises (see Legals p. 133). Where any part of your price is left outstanding it is imperative that you look to protect yourself, e.g. by requiring the buyer to pay money into a deposit or escrow account, or giving a guarantee supported by some meaningful collateral. Remember that in the absence of the buyer paying the money into such an account, your agreement to defer payment is financing their purchase!

Bottom line: cash on completion is king.

Preparing Your Business for Sale

In much the same way as your house never looks better than the day it's placed on the market, it is sensible to carry out some checks and cleaning of your business before pressing the sale button. There are two main reasons for this: the first is to address any issues which may otherwise have a negative impact on your price, and the second is to ensure there is nothing lurking in the undergrowth which might delay or derail the sale process.

The key is to uncover any problems or weaknesses before your buyer does, as it will leverage any issues to their advantage, e.g. by reducing the price – particularly if matters come to light late in the sale process – or by them holding back some of the price until the matter is resolved.

Advisers

Having made the decision to sell, the first step is to engage experienced advisers. These will include an accountant (not necessarily your auditors) or corporate finance adviser and lawyers. It is important to have an engagement letter drawn up that deals clearly with fees. These are commonly fixed or 'capped' at a particular amount and advisers may agree arrangements where part of their fee is conditional on completion or upon the sale price achieving a particular level.

There is a popular quotation (my father claims it, but I happen to know Oscar Wilde got there first) that refers to the dangers for the man who knows the price of everything and the value of nothing. Seldom is this more apt than when choosing the people to guide you through this process. Do not confuse the two – it is vital that your advisers have a track record in this arena as they can influence both the price you get and whether the deal happens at all. In terms of costs, as a crude rule of thumb you should not expect to spend more than 5 per cent of your proceeds in adviser fees.

Tax planning

Most sellers will understandably wish to minimise the amount of tax they suffer on their hard-earned proceeds. Tax avoidance (unlike tax evasion) is perfectly legal, but you should settle any restructuring which needs to be carried out before engaging with your buyer.

Getting ready

Once you have carried out checks on your business to identify any issues which could adversely affect the price or process, it would then be helpful to start collating information in files in preparation for the buyer's own pre-contract enquiries. To minimise disruption to your business, consider whether the documents can be assembled on a dedicated website created for the purpose (aka 'data room').

Information memorandum

Your advisers may prepare a 'taster' document giving interested parties information about your business. This should be subject to a confidentiality agreement preventing recipients from misusing information about your business that they might receive during the process. The safe course? Be selective about the timing of the release of commercially sensitive information; the later the better.

Identify your buyer

This is typically the next step in the process. To reiterate, the ideal is to create and maintain a competitive tension for as long as possible. At some point you will usually have to run with one party exclusively, but the shorter that period, and the later in the process, the better.

Some general observations: While most business owners will say that they know the likely buyers of their business, the reality is often quite different. Experienced advisers who know your sector will often have thoughts and connections which hadn't occurred to you.

On that note a word of caution: There are numerous brokers in the market who will offer to sell your business for you. While brokerages offer an excellent network and will ensure that few stones are left unturned in finding a potential buyer, indiscriminate marketing of your business can be counterproductive, particularly if unsuccessful. Separately, do not underestimate the value of having an impartial adviser sitting alongside you whose objective is your interests rather than completion of your deal at any cost.

The range of potential buyers is diverse and should be the subject of your early conversations with your advisers. By way of example, the buyer could be a competitor or a supplier, or a much larger corporate operating in your sector; alternatively the buyer could be your existing management team (alone or in combination with an experienced outsider) or for that matter a financial buyer such as a private equity firm. The important point is that each buyer will have a different approach and pose different challenges; your advisers will be key to ensuring that your deal is delivered and that you are properly protected.

The key factors to consider when looking at a potential buyer are:

— **Structure:** are they offering cash?
— **Funding:** do they have the money?
— **Certainty:** how quickly can they proceed?
— **Liability:** what level of protection will they expect from you? Put another way, what residual liability to the buyer will you have after the deal? (Once you've received your money you don't want to have to hand it back to satisfy claims.)

You may also be concerned about the buyer's plans for your business and your staff. This is all before you consider the price being offered, though sometimes there is a trade-off between getting top dollar and these other factors.

Legals

This is the point at which lawyers are engaged by you and the buyer. Some context: the entire approach taken by the buyer and seller to this aspect, and that of their lawyers, can be summarised by **the four Rs**. For you as the seller the issues are **receipt** and **retention** of your sale proceeds, and for the buyer it's all about **risk** and **recovery**. Every negotiation issue can be traced back to one or more of these principles.

The role of your lawyers typically starts with negotiating **heads of terms** (aka memorandum of understanding, offer letter or letter of intent). These are signed with your proposed buyer once the main commercial terms of your deal are settled. As the heads are not legally binding they should be brief and restricted to key matters such as price, payment terms and timetable.

The buyer will want a period during which you will not negotiate with anyone else for the sale of your business ('exclusivity') – given that the buyer will be incurring significant costs, this is not an unreasonable request. The period should be short, e.g. eight weeks, and you should consider taking a non-refundable deposit from the buyer as a gesture of their commitment (particularly as the buyer can otherwise walk away from your deal with impunity).

If the buyer has not already signed a confidentiality agreement then the protection of your commercial information should also be addressed in the heads and made legally binding.

The next step is the buyer's due diligence or 'DD' –
in effect, a health check on your business. This can be
time-consuming and, confidentiality permitting, you
should delegate the task of collating the replies to a few
trusted senior individuals, agree the scope of the DD in
advance and a timetable, and stick to it.

The principal legal agreement is known as the 'share
(or business) purchase agreement' and is normally
prepared by the buyer's lawyers. This will deal with:

— **Terms for the sale** such as the price, its calculation
and when and how it is to be paid.
— **Warranties and indemnities** to be given by you as
the seller (see below).
— **Restrictive covenants** to be given by you (restrictions
preserving the goodwill of the target business by
preventing you from competing with it for a period).

A word on warranties and indemnities. This is the area
where you are at risk of handing your sale proceeds
back to the buyer. Warranties are statements by you as
seller about your business and intended to reassure the
buyer. If they are incorrect, then the buyer can claim
financial compensation (it will argue it has overpaid for
your business). An indemnity, on the other hand, usually
addresses a known risk and is a promise by the seller to
reimburse the buyer if that event happens.

Tips: your warranties should be qualified by a full disclosure
to the buyer of anything inconsistent with those statements;
when selling shares, a deliberate untrue statement or
dishonest concealment of material facts can be a criminal
offence; your financial liability should be limited and the
time for the buyer to bring claims restricted.

As a rule of thumb, a well-run sale process should take no longer than six to eight weeks from the signing of heads of terms (emphasis here on 'well-run'!)

Lastly, some words of wisdom about the sale process:

— **Deal fatigue:** the process can become protracted so remember your day job and 'keep your eyes on the ball'. Deterioration in performance can ultimately affect price and the success of your deal.

— **Price chipping:** beware last-minute price negotiations by the buyer. This may be for genuine unexpected reasons, but a well-run sale process should reduce the scope for this significantly. Always be prepared to walk away.

— **Tyre kickers:** take care in the release of commercially sensitive information during early stages of negotiations. Beware those who are more interested in learning about your business than buying it.

— **Confidentiality:** the whispers that your business is for sale can have an unsettling effect. As far as possible, key personnel, customers and suppliers should be kept in the loop – one way or another they are all likely to be crucial not just to your business but also the success of your sale process.

— **Negotiations:** your advisers should shield you from the detail so that you and your buyer are involved in as few face-to-face meetings as possible. A constructive approach to the buyer's issues and an understanding of its perspective can save negotiations from becoming emotive and keep the process on track. Early face-to-face introductions between advisers and principals can help, as can encouraging all parties but particularly the lawyers to view the process as a project rather than a battle.

— **Advisers:** good lines of communication between you and your advisers are key. They must talk to each other and your accountants or corporate finance advisers should take responsibility for managing the overall process. Above all, they should remember that they are facilitators – the process is not about them.

Summary

The sale of your business can often be a drawn-out and complex affair. It is imperative to have experienced advisers on board from the outset. A well-run process preserves value for you and improves the chances of success for your deal. Choose your advisers carefully, don't neglect the day job, and always be prepared to walk away if the deal strays too far from your objectives.

Conclusion

Whatever the background to your decision to start your own business, it will certainly be one of the bravest and most challenging you have made. It can also be the most exciting and rewarding thing you ever do.

Being your own boss is a hugely liberating experience but can equally be a lonely place; this book is on your side. My hope and intention in writing this guide is not that you become a legal expert but that you are aware of the issues involved. It doesn't necessarily provide the bridge across every bear pit, but hopefully tells you where and how deep it is, how to navigate your way around it, or simply soften your fall!

If there is one consistent piece of advice I have shared with all entrepreneur clients it is that while nothing you do is risk free there is a lot you can do to reduce the likelihood of mishap. There is no substitute for starting out with your eyes wide open.

The central theme of this book has been protection, and specifically protection through building strong foundations for your business from the outset.

So let's recap on some key messages:

From a financial perspective key issues for you will be managing your cash flow effectively and good supply chain management (aka buying and selling) to ensure customer satisfaction.

At the operational level there are a number of issues to address:

Business structure

We know why getting this right matters – to limit your exposure. For me, this is straightforward: limited liability is the key and that means a limited company or a Limited Liability Partnership (of these two, companies are by far the most common). Some dislike the administration and transparency which comes with that territory, and tax can be an issue, but personally this is one of the more straightforward decisions. A private company limited by shares ticks substantially all the boxes.

Website and e-commerce

We have touched on the regulatory aspects of online trading and the key messages are:

— **Website terms and conditions of business:** properly prepared these should go a long way to ensuring your compliance with the various E-commerce Regulations. It's definitely worth engaging a lawyer, particularly where you are dealing with consumers.

— **Website content:** make sure you have the necessary permissions, particularly if you are using imagery or other media belonging to others.

— **Data protection:** having appropriate privacy and cookie policies in place is essential.

Raising finance

There are a variety of sources and types available to startups, from government grants to bank loans and private equity investment. The trick is knowing where to look and understanding what the different types of funding mean for you and your business. When it comes to equity investment, remember: firstly, there is often little room for negotiation, so pick your battles carefully; secondly, in choosing your investor, look beyond the cash.

Trading contracts

Every dealing your business has with its customers and suppliers will be governed by a contract. Your objective is to ensure that as far as possible you control and/or influence the terms of that contract. At the very least you should have your own standard conditions of sale to regulate the contract between you and your buyers.

Staff

Recruiting and retaining the right people is key. Remember that the hiring and firing processes can be a minefield for the unwary and you should protect your business with proper contracts of employment for your staff from the outset.

Intellectual property

We looked at the different types of IP, where they might arise in your business and how to protect and exploit them. Although the registration process can be a time-consuming and expensive exercise, failure to protect key intellectual property rights can be considerably more damaging.

There are plenty of risks in business that you can do nothing about (from the state of the global economy to unexpected failures of key customers or suppliers), so at the very least you should protect your business against those risks which are within your control. This means addressing those areas we have touched on throughout this book. To repeat, nothing in business is risk free and if it were there would be little profit in it. The secret is reducing the scope for those risks to happen, which means laying secure foundations for your business and giving yourself the opportunity to spot the pitfalls and protect yourself against them.

I hope this book goes some way to help you achieve those objectives. Good luck!

Resources

A few links and websites which you might find helpful:

Business Structures

www.gov.uk/business-legal-structures

www.companieshouse.gov.uk

Websites and domain names

www.nominet.org.uk

www.networksolutions.com

www.gov.uk/search-for-trademark

Data Protection (websites and e-commerce)

www.ico.org.uk

Intellectual Property

www.ipo.gov.uk

Funding

www.ukbusinessangelsassociation.org.uk

www.bvca.co.uk

www.british-business-bank.co.uk

VAT

www.hmrc.gov.uk/vat

About the Author

Johnathan Rees is a company commercial lawyer.
He has more than 25 years' experience of advising a
wide range of clients from entrepreneurs to large
owner-managed businesses, international corporations,
banks and private equity institutions.

Having started his career in the City with an international
law firm he subsequently became a partner in large
provincial firms based in Manchester and Bristol.

He advises on matters ranging from business startups
and commercial contracts to raising finance, joint ventures
and mergers and acquisitions.

Welsh and a keen sportsman, Johnathan's first-class rugby
career saw him lying on physio tables at London Welsh,
Bath and Headingley.

He lives and works in London.

Thanks

Like many ideas this book was inspired by a few beers; on this occasion late one bitterly cold spring evening in a pub in a field near Cardigan Bay. It turned into a significant project for one man and without the help and encouragement of a number of people it would not have happened.

Thanks to David and Clare Hieatt for inviting me to speak at the Do Lectures and giving me the opportunity to write my book.

Thanks to Miranda West of Do Books for her guidance and relentless enthusiasm, and together with copy-editor Ian Allen, for their professionalism and transforming my words into a proper book.

Thanks to Lana Elie, the talented Founder and CEO of Floom Limited, for sharing her experience of the crowdfunding process.

Last but not least, thanks to my firm Joelson for their help and support with this book and to Alex Tutty at the law firm Sheridans.

Index

admin, essential 106–17
    accounting 107, 108
    banking 110–11
    companies 108–9, 114–15
    filing 108
    insurance 111–12
    Limited Liability Partnerships (LLP) 109, 115
    partnerships and sole traders 110
    small companies 109
    tax 108–9
    trading disclosures 114–16
    VAT 112–14
agents 74, 75
Apple 35, 36
articles of association 22
assets 13, 16, 18, 20, 21, 26, 33, 34, 38, 52, 108, 109, 119, 121, 123–4

Branson, Richard 14
business angels 53
Business Bank 53, 137
business structures 13–24, 134

Companies Act 109
Companies House 40, 108, 109, 110
contracts 64-6
cookies 28, 30, 31, 81, 84–5
crowdfunding 54, 55
customers 67–72

data controller 28–9, 85
Data Protection Act, 1998 (DPA) 28, 85
directors 16, 17, 18, 19, 22, 24, 59, 94, 95, 108, 109, 111–12, 114, 115
distributors 74, 75

e-commerce 25, 73, 78–86, 90, 134–5
    background 80
    compliance 86

Data Protection Act 85
distance selling regulations 81, 83–4
e-commerce regulations 81–3
privacy regulations and cookies 81, 84–5
regulations 80–8, 134–5
spam 83
trading disclosures 85
employees 38, 39, 87, 94–5, 96, 101, 102, 103–4, 105, 108, 109, 110, 111
Enterprise Investment Scheme 54
Equality Act, 2010 97
'equity gap' 10
European Patent Convention (EPC) 43
European Patent Office (EPO) 43
European Union (EU) 41, 42, 43–4, 75, 81, 112

Facebook 80, 87, 123
finance, raising 9, 14, 23, 24, 39, 47–61, 135
    banks 51–2
    business angels 53
    choosing your equity investor 59–60
    corporate venturers 54
    crowdfunding 54, 55
    debt (or loan) 48, 49, 51–2
    equity 48, 49, 50, 53–4, 56–8
    friends and family 53
    government schemes 53
    government sources 54
    peer-to-peer lending 53
    sources of funding 51–4
    types of funding 48–50
    venture capitalists 54
Financial Conduct Authority 55

hiring 97–100
    adverts 98
    candidate selection 98
    contract 100

discrimination 97
health & safety 100
interview 99
offer 99–100
process 97–8
staff procedures 100
HMRC 96, 104, 110, 113, 114, 137

incorporated business structures 14–20
Information Commissioner's
Office (ICO) 28, 85, 137
Intellectual Property Office
(IPO) 27, 41, 43, 44, 137
intellectual property (IP) rights 27, 32–46,
    67, 88, 89, 135–6
    confidential information 38–9, 44–5
    copyright 38
    design rights 37
    enforcing your 45
    exploiting your 48
    how to register your 41–5
    ownership of 39–40
    patents 35, 36, 42–4
    registered designs 36, 37, 44
    trademarks 36, 41–2
investors 10, 14, 24, 42, 44, 47, 48, 49, 50,
    52, 54, 56, 57, 58, 59, 60, 61, 135

licensee 75–6
Limited Liability Partnership (LLP):
    admin 19, 109, 115
    building your team 94
    business structure 14, 18–20
    business vehicle, setting up your
    22–3, 24
    liability 18–19
    management 19
    ownership 19
    raising finance 48, 52
    selling your business 121

tax 20
Linkedin 87

Madrid Protocol 42
memorandum of association 22

National Minimum Wage (NMW) 95, 96
non-disclosure agreements (NDAs) 44–5

Office for Harmonisation in the Internal
    Market (OHIM) 42
online trading see e-commerce
owner-managed business 17, 122, 138

partnership:
    admin 107, 110, 115
    business structure 14, 21
    raising finance and 48
    selling your business and 121
    setting up a 23
Patent Co-operation Treaty (PCT) 43
private limited company 134
    admin 17, 109, 113, 114–15
    business structure 14, 15–18
    liability 16–17
    raising finance and 48, 52
    selling your business and 120–2
    setting up your 22–4
    tax 18, 113

Registrar of Companies 17, 19, 22

Seed Enterprise Investment Scheme 54
selling your business 118–31
    advisers 125
    information memorandum 126
    legals 128–30
    partial exits 122
    preparations 124–5
    sale processes 120, 130–1

sale structures 120–1
tax planning 125–6
value 123
shareholders 16, 17, 18, 22, 94, 103, 108, 109, 121, 122
SMEs (small to medium enterprises) 53
social media 79, 87–9, 90, 98
    employees 87
    protections 88–9
    risks 87
    third parties 87
sole trader:
    admin 110–11, 114, 115
    business structure 14, 20–1, 23
    raising finance 48, 52
    selling your business 121
staff incentives 103–5, 135
sub-contracting 72
suppliers 72–3

tax:
    accounting and 107, 108–9, 110
    business structure and 14, 15, 18, 20, 21, 23, 24, 134
    corporation tax 18, 44, 108
    customers and 67
    employees and 93, 103, 104
    incentives available to investors 24
    IPR and 44
    raising finance and 51, 54
    selling your business and 121, 125–6
    VAT see VAT
    website and 82
team, building your 92–105
termination of employment 102–3
trademarks 36, 41–2
Twitter 87

UK Business Angels Association 53
unincorporated businesses 14, 20

VAT 82, 112–14, 117, 137

website, establishing your 25–31
    business information 30
    comments posted on your 88, 89
    content 27–8
    cookies 28, 30, 31, 81, 84–5
    data 28–9
    direct sales through 73, 79, 80, 82, 84–5, 86
    domain name 26–7, 40
    legal framework 25–6
    links 29
    privacy regulations and cookies 84–5
    staff using 87
    terms and conditions of business 30–1, 134–5
WHOIS database 27
World Intellectual Property Organisation (WIPO) 42, 43